Advance praise for *Winning at C*

"This is a good read. The authors allude mation is commoditized, access comman mation economy is replaced by a colla ɔmy, and intellectual capital is superseded by relationship tal. That future is happening today."
—**Antony Brydon**, CEO, Visible Path Corporation

"Collaboration is critical to knowledge-worker performance. The authors go well beyond the previous injunctions to 'play nice together', and identify ways to improve processes and make money through collaborative commerce."
—**Thomas H. Davenport**, President's Distinguished Professor of Information Technology and Management, Babson College

"Whether you are an innovator or a forward-looking executive at an industry leader, *Winning at Collaboration Commerce* will be an essential resource for you. Knowledge and reputation flow through existing business relationship networks faster than ever before, which creates opportunities for reinventing how business gets done in dozens of knowledge-intensive industries."
—**Konstantin Guericke**, Founder, Linked In

"In the past decade, companies achieved tremendous efficiency gains by streamlining their internal processes. Today's forward-thinking companies are using a collaborative commerce focus to achieve even greater efficiencies by optimizing their business networks and relationships beyond the firewall. *Winning at Collaboration Commerce* provides examples of how companies are using collaborative commerce to reach new customers, speed products to market, and outperform their competitors."
—**Subrah Iyar**, CEO, WebEx Communications

"RBC Financial Group is continually looking through what the authors call the collaborative lens when we develop or enhance our business to improve the client experience. The authors have done an outstanding job in highlighting real-world examples of how c-commerce can take you to new heights when you're ready

WITHDRAWN

to look beyond the walls of your organization and partner with the best."

—**Martin Lippert**, Vice Chairman and Head, Global Technology and Operations, RBC Financial Group

"Winning, in general, is getting harder and harder as the world becomes flatter. But this book contains many crucial insights into the fundamental changes that are required to master a sustainable edge in this emerging global economy. The book is not just theory. It contains great wisdom on just how important collaboration with partners is becoming and then how to implement a collaborative fabric within and across ecosystems. Yes, the game is changing, but with the lenses of collaborative process networks there are new ways to achieve strategic advantage."

—**John Seely Brown**, Former Chief Scientist, Xerox Corporation; Co-Author, *The Only Sustainable Edge*

"A great way to get started on thinking about the implications of collaboration, and more importantly a way to take action before the networked economy passes you by."

—**Dave Snowden**, CEO and Founder, The Cynefin Centre

WINNING AT
COLLABORATION
COMMERCE

WINNING AT COLLABORATION COMMERCE

THE NEXT COMPETITIVE ADVANTAGE

Heidi Collins
Cindy Gordon
José Cláudio Terra

ELSEVIER

AMSTERDAM • BOSTON • HEIDELBERG
LONDON • NEW YORK • OXFORD • PARIS
SAN DIEGO • SAN FRANCISCO • SINGAPORE
SYDNEY • TOKYO
Butterworth-Heinemann is an imprint of Elsevier

Elsevier Butterworth–Heinemann
30 Corporate Drive, Suite 400, Burlington, MA 01803, USA
Linacre House, Jordan Hill, Oxford OX2 8DP, UK

Copyright © 2006, Heidi Collins, Cindy Gordon, José Cláudio Terra.
All rights reserved.

No part of this publication may be reproduced, stored in a retrieval system,
or transmitted in any form or by any means, electronic, mechanical,
photocopying, recording, or otherwise, without the prior written permission
of the publisher.

Permissions may be sought directly from Elsevier's Science & Technology
Rights Department in Oxford, UK: phone: (+44) 1865 843830, fax:
(+44) 1865 853333, e-mail: permissions@elsevier.co.uk. You may also
complete your request on-line via the Elsevier homepage (http://elsevier.com),
by selecting "Customer Support" and then "Obtaining Permissions."

Recognizing the importance of preserving what has been written, Elsevier
prints its books on acid-free paper whenever possible.

Library of Congress Cataloging-in-Publication Data
Collins, Heidi.
    Winning at collaboration commerce : the next competitive advantage /
Heidi Collins, Cindy Gordon, José Cláudio Terra.
      p. cm.
    Includes bibliographical references and index.
    ISBN 0-7506-7817-8
    1. Strategic planning.   2. Organizational change.   3. Management.
I. Gordon, Cindy.   II. Terra, José Cláudio Cyrineu.   III. Title.
HD30.28.C64315 2005
658—dc22

                                                          2005052408

British Library Cataloguing-in-Publication Data
A catalogue record for this book is available from the British Library.

ISBN 13: 978-0-7506-7817-9
ISBN 10: 0-7506-7817-8

For information on all Elsevier Butterworth–Heinemann publications
visit our Web site at www.books.elsevier.com

Printed in the United States of America
05 06 07 08 09 10   10 9 8 7 6 5 4 3 2 1

Working together to grow
libraries in developing countries

www.elsevier.com | www.bookaid.org | www.sabre.org

ELSEVIER   BOOK AID   Sabre Foundation
            International

"The most important, and indeed the truly unique, contribution of management in the 20th century was the fiftyfold increase in the productivity of the MANUAL WORKER in manufacturing. The most important contribution management needs to make in the 21st century is similarly to increase the productivity of KNOWLEDGE WORK and the KNOWLEDGE WORKER."

—Peter Drucker

CONTENTS

3

C-COMMERCE FRAMEWORK   32

PART II   MAKING IT HAPPEN: THE C-COMMERCE DIMENSIONS   49

4

THE GOVERNANCE DIMENSION   54

5

THE STRATEGY DIMENSION   66

6

THE PROCESS DIMENSION   85

7

THE INFORMATION TECHNOLOGY INFRASTRUCTURE DIMENSION 107

8

THE PEOPLE DIMENSION 133

9

THE CULTURE AND CHANGE DIMENSION   157

10

THE MEASUREMENT DIMENSION   182

PART III   THE IMPLEMENTATION PATH   203

11

C-COMMERCE: GETTING STARTED   205

12

C-COMMERCE QUICK REVIEW   219

APPENDIX: C-COMMERCE INTELLIGENCE ASSESSMENT   231

PREFACE

What is collaboration commerce? What are the possibilities that collaboration commerce will generate in organizations? What are the implications if an organization does not pursue collaboration commerce? This book aims to answer these questions.

There is a rapidly emerging, dominant voice in business strategy, organizational theory, information technology, and economics that traditional business models are quickly evolving. The dominant voice is networks of collaboration, and highly adaptive business models create new ecosystems. Collaboration commerce, or c-commerce, is the new management strategy for helping organizations adapt and thrive in complex and often chaotic business environments.

We were inspired to pursue knowledge-worker competencies aimed at optimizing innovation and growth. There is no question that the traditional approaches to governance, strategy, business processes, technologies, people, culture, and measurement systems are not meeting accelerated marketplace and consumer demands. Individuals and information in our organizations are not self-contained, and knowledge workers are most innovative when permitted to be self-forming, collaborative networks of people, content, and technologies.

C-commerce is a participatory approach to business, leveraging social capital that is built on trust, reciprocity, and networks. There are aspects of customer capital theory based on personas and market boundaries that are becoming more transparent. Business strategy theory emphasizes the importance of leadership and governance in driving successful change in an organization and throughout the value chain. Market fundamentals and information technology theory stress real-time, adaptive, and collaborative systems to meet work group knowledge-sharing requirements. Our experiences as business executives, venture capitalists, academics, researchers, and writers drove us to identify a logical way to look at innovation and the growth of industries and organizations.

This book has been a journey of collaboration and recognizes the reflexive nature of human beings—their self-reflection, responsiveness and adaptiveness, and need for self-actualization. Too many of our business strategies and organizational models have become suffocating and rigid; c-commerce is about taking advantage of what is already happening around us and incorporating it into new business strategies. For example, the personal information on the Internet makes certain that none of us will ever have to go on a "blind" date. Knowledge workers have become slaves to e-mail management, voice mail, instant messaging, and the countless interruptions the work environment supports. We believe using collaborative capabilities to combine the information available and the ability to better use and integrate technology with the appropriate organizational model create the next competitive advantage for nations, industries, firms, and organizations, both profit and nonprofit.

We hope that by reading this book you will learn how to win at c-commerce. Writing it has been the fulfillment of a vision inspired by Peter Drucker, whom we dedicate this book to with admiration and respect. Knowledge workers remain our current and future economy in a world that continues to hold back the reflexive and highly complex adaptive characteristics of knowledge flow. We are excited to introduce c-commerce as the path that will inspire the new thoughts, reflection, and renewal that are critical for change.

ACKNOWLEDGMENTS

Edwin Schlossberg once said, "The skill of writing is to create a context in which other people can think." As a writing team we were able to collaborate on ideas, shape them into new thoughts, and expand them into c-commerce. This book is designed to provide the context needed to inspire ideas and help leaders understand the business imperative to act on c-commerce. Without all the wonderful people who shared their new ideas and gave us access to brilliance, we would not have been able to complete the project. To our past and future readers—your joy to learn makes all of this worthwhile.

The professional and qualified team at Elsevier made this project come to life. We were honored to work directly with Karen Maloney, Dennis McGonagle, Heather Furrow, and Julie Louis. The book reflects the combined collaborative work of our personal commitments and individual talents. We are all better for the experience.

Heidi recognizes: The glory of God. This book was written with the support of my husband and son, Jeff Collins and C. James Collins, who provide the love and support that allow me to pursue my dreams and success as an author. It is their belief in me that continues to inspire my work and achievements. Their continued support, encouragement, and understanding made the collaboration commerce project possible.

Cindy recognizes: my husband, Perry Muhlbier, and children Jessica and Bryce for their endless patience in allowing me the freedom to channel my creative energies while balancing business and personal life. Their gifts of love are my heaven. To my parents, Norma and Benny, your encouragement to reach new heights is in my DNA, and your gift of life makes all this possible. To Heidi and Cláudio, your tenacity and goodness have only made me more humble while working with your collaborating spirits.

Cláudio recognizes: My wife, Janine, and my son, Luc. This book was written during Luc's first year. What an amazing year! I feel humbled by the beauty and love that a new baby inspires and by the amazing strength and love of my wife, Janine. Thanks for helping me make time to write this book. You are the best! The TerraForum team, and Dr. Rupert Brown in particular, were also incredibly helpful in providing great research material, feedback, detailed editing, and formatting. Working with Cindy and Heidi across three different countries was a powerful collaboration experience. I believe that we all learned as much from our research as from our co-writing experience. Cheers to collaboration!

PART I

THE
FUNDAMENTALS

1

C-COMMERCE SHIFT

This book addresses a major business and economic shift that is rapidly under way and is being led by business leaders and forward thinkers. This fundamental shift is about the emergence of what we define as *collaboration commerce*. C-commerce is a combination of disruptive and collaborative business models; the integration of new mind-sets, values, and technologies to achieve higher levels of collaboration; and innovation among individuals, firms, and geographies.

As we started this book, we realized that c-commerce requires deep and simultaneous commitment and change across a number of areas: governance, strategy, process design, information technology (IT), people management, culture, and metrics. We wanted to provide leaders with a good understanding of the importance of this fundamental business shift and also a practical operational context for this rapidly evolving area. The ultimate goal of this book is to help prepare leaders to develop their strategies and migration plans to take advantage of collaborative business models.

An important characteristic of the drive toward c-commerce is the undisputed value of network effects on the ability of an organization to grow exponentially and to generate above-average returns. Collaborative networks create new value possibilities for the whole ecosystem of enterprises involved in a value chain. The issue is not about economies of scale or scope; it is about leverage—how every player in the ecosystem can leverage each other's information, knowledge, skills, contacts, and brand into multiple win-win situations. In the past, companies shared mainly physical resources, whereas now the key is to share knowledge, which can build more intelligent organizations or, from a network perspective, build a "collective intelligence."

How fact-based is this book? There are clear indications of the importance of c-commerce everywhere for those who are prepared to spot them. Yet, there is no single indicator of the benefits or the trends associated with c-commerce. This book includes many important caselets (mini-cases) that support our assessment of c-commerce, and we have assembled insights from multiple sources and presented facts that validate our main thesis: Increased collaboration is a fact of life in science, business, and markets. It is the next competitive advantage, and we are convinced that collaboration is the root of innovation practices.

THE EARLY ADOPTERS

Although these changes are rapidly taking place, the ideas, frameworks, and attributes outlined in this book are not yet commonplace. They are a mix of our intuition and experiences and are supported by research of early adopters of c-commerce. We also highlight relevant trends in innovative software solutions based on social network concepts. Fundamentally, this book is about the inevitable changes that will occur as new generations enter the workforce either to build new forms of enterprises or to reform existing ones.

So who is leading the pack in c-commerce? Are they high-tech companies or old industries? Big or small? From developed or developing countries? We can say with a good degree of confidence that we have been able to find interesting examples from all sorts of industries, sizes, and places. Both industry titans such as Microsoft and unlikely organizations such as Sugar Cane Cooperatives in Brazil are sourcing information, knowledge, innovation, and partners everywhere across the globe. As they do this and we start paying attention, we realize that examples abound everywhere.

Seeing c-commerce in action requires special lenses and filters. We hope that this book will help business leaders to change the filter they use to see the world and to begin to rethink their business strategies from a deeper relationship and collaborative lens.

C-COMMERCE AND COMPETITIVE ADVANTAGE

In an economy in which information is a raw material and ideas are the currency of knowledge exchange, quality conversations and interactions are where knowledge workers are able to share and refine their thinking in order to create new products and services. This book is not about innovation management, yet it became very clear when we finished our research and laid out the structure of this book that networks are where innovation is cultivated. If you believe, as we do, that competition is increasingly based on innovation, it follows that the ability to operate and lead in collaboration is key to growth and sustainability.

Knowledge, know-how, markets, and technologies were much easier to protect just a decade ago. Now, even much smaller players can quickly overtake leading companies by assembling skills, resources, focus, and market knowledge through critical collaboration. Take the example of mobile telecommunications. Motorola was the dominant and pioneer player in this market for much of the 1980s and early 1990s. But its global leadership was quickly eroded by much smaller players, despite its clear technological leadership. Its ivory-tower, centralized research and development, technology-driven approach reflected old-style business concepts. Nokia and Samsung were more open to the development of more intimate relationships with consumers and also other telecommunications companies. Now they are the global leaders. Coincidence? We think not.

Revolutions are often hard to see because they are not driven by incumbents or mainstream businesses. Open-source software development is a good example. The model, practices, and behaviors were not initiated by leading software companies, but by communities of developers collaborating informally, through new processes and behaviors. The study of this phenomenon led incumbent software developers to begin to open up and to think more broadly of their ecosystem. In fact, other industries have been affected and even the traditional scientific community is rethinking its secular traditions of intellectual property, publishing channels, knowledge sharing, and collaboration practices.

In the c-commerce context, the next competitive advantage is focused to a great extent on relationship capital (reputation, trust, and the breadth of our networks). Achieving competitive advantage will be based on the trust-making and collaboration capabilities of partners, vendors, customers, supplies, and employees to build value. Many organizations have not realized the implication that the next competitive wave resides in what makes us innately "human"—our continued quest to seek collaborative dialogues, develop trust, and have reciprocal experiences. These are all fundamental cornerstones of c-commerce.

The Internet has created a world of chaotic competition in which customers have more choices and suppliers have more opportunities; this is driving the most fundamental change in businesses to create more agile and highly focused enterprises that execute in or near real time. Enterprises in the next decade will need to follow the motto used by ancient Olympians: "Citius, altius, fortius" ("Faster, higher, braver").

- *Faster* as more and more enterprises strive for real-time collaboration capabilities that remove latency from processes in support of more interconnected business models, which demand accurate and timely information.
- *Higher* return on investment and earning per share via cost cutting, modified business models, and a renewed focus on core competencies.
- *Braver* in the form of collaboration, customer and supplier portals, marketplaces, and fundamentally more open business models and application architectures.

C-COMMERCE AND TIMING

Time is of the essence and perhaps the most valuable resource for knowledge workers and knowledge-intensive businesses. In this context, speed of resolution, speed of innovation, and speed to market are often key drivers for c-commerce. In a global economy in which competitors are constantly on the lookout and are mobilized to penetrate new markets and respond rapidly to any move, the winners tend to be those that understand the power of collaboration for gaining speed. In many advanced markets, speed now means real time!

Agility is the name of the game in a world of increasingly shorter high-margin time windows in many industries. Organizations that understand the effectiveness of collaboration are more likely to leverage their core competencies and take advantage of emerging market opportunities outside their mainstream lines of business through collaborative initiatives with different partners.

Real-time collaborative enterprise synergies require a complex collaborative ecosystem and a multilayered value chain. Supply chain collaboration has become a broad umbrella term that covers engineering, buying and selling, inventory management, and schedule synchronization. Stakeholders can visualize complete information across the entire product cycle in real time, from design to final product sales. With full product and process knowledge, they can seamlessly work in concert.

C-Commerce and the Information Infrastructure

To support this new level of collaboration across departments, firms, and geographies, organizations should also pay attention to the evolving landscape of collaboration software. A good example of c-commerce software is the next generation of software that identifies people as branded profiles and tracks all their information exchanges, buying attributes, and patterns of interaction through their network activity. This kind of tracking creates a real-time business dynamic in which transparency and collaboration form new capabilities and reputation metrics.

New forms of collaborative intelligence solutions are being created to support executives' decision making. An interesting scenario illustrates this point. Imagine a senior vice president of sales and business development who is in a major sales cycle. One of her products requires a new channel partner in another country, yet she has no contacts in the other country. She could simply specify her requirements, and the relational and reputational engines (known as six-degree-of-separation software) would pinpoint her best options for business collaborators and also tell her who in her current network already knows these potential partners so she can avoid a cold call.

This scenario is already here. One of the hottest venture capital areas is social networking software integrated with customer relationship management and supply chain management platforms to create collaboration commerce software foundations. Driving this scenario and development is the realization of the value of relationship capital as a key measure of intangible asset and market value both for individuals and firms.

We recognize the importance of this new breed of software and dedicate a complete chapter of the book to information technology. IT, however, is only the tip of the iceberg. In fact, many industry pundits and innovators say that, besides integration issues, change management is the key challenge in most large software deployments, particularly those that involve implementation of portals, content management, virtual workspaces, and business-to-business marketplaces.

INTERNAL AND EXTERNAL COLLABORATION

Although much of this book focuses on the external aspects of collaboration, we also delve into many aspects of internal collaboration or knowledge management. As our research evolved, it became quite clear that it is difficult for any organization to jump onto the c-commerce bandwagon unless it has already dealt with related issues internally. Many companies are totally unprepared to take advantage of collaborative business models. Their service models do not reflect the depth of collaboration and spirit required to secure long-term customer loyalty while employee leadership practices remain gridlocked in controlling and bullying behaviors in many of the Fortune 500 companies. These generate more fear-based and protectionism behaviors than authentic and collaborative knowledge-sharing behaviors.

We have been involved with knowledge management (KM) for the last 10 years and have seen that companies that have embraced KM fully are more prepared for c-commerce. These are companies that are already focusing on their core competencies, fostering organizational learning, valuing and making their intellectual capital more explicit, instilling visions around the importance of knowledge sharing, and building more open and collaborative IT infrastructures. These are crucial consider-ations and factors for supporting the move toward c-commerce.

LEADING THE CHANGE

We argue in this book that to compete in this new world order, leaders will need to understand the value relationships among many diverse stakeholders—distributors, manufacturers, cus-tomers, suppliers, partners, and employees—and to understand how Internet and trade exchange/marketplace models can improve their business efficiency to create a super-efficient pro-duction with real-time intelligence at all business layers.

One of the most important recommendations of this book is for chief executives and strategic planning executives to rethink their business models and to consider how they interact with all their key stakeholders. They need an explicit model or even a scorecard of how collaboration permeates these relationships. In many cases, this will not be a quantitative, financial metric. We believe, however, that leading businesses attuned to current trends and economic realities will increasingly pay as much attention to their "collaboration index" as they pay to their quarterly results. We explore this in more depth in the third part of this book.

How important is c-commerce and how soon should busi-ness leaders start paying attention to it? Is it coming to their doorsteps anytime soon? We are convinced that we are right in the eye of the storm. The speed with which this is occurring has reminded us of the saying, "Revolution is just evolution that happened when you were not looking." As we said earlier, if business leaders wear new lenses, they will see that c-commerce is penetrating many different channels of everyday life. People just have to check, for instance, on how their kids might be doing their homework. Smart kids not only look at (virtual) encyclopedias, they may enter a virtual collaboration space and gather information from primary sources across the globe.

One does not have to look away for long to be caught off guard by a new revolution. Leaders will either grasp this next competitive advantage or react too late to compete effectively. In some respects, people and firms are becoming DNA nodes or vessels of knowledge, which are streaming in real time and forming smart diodes, which cluster into "relationship knowledge exchange flows" and then reform as dynamically as they are created. Each DNA diode will have a profile and will have a historical reputational handshake, which will either attract or repel acceptance for a c-commerce exchange.

As humanity's problems, challenges, and goals become increasingly more complex—dealing with global warming, deciphering the human genome, exploring space—the need for collective intelligence can only increase in importance. Current advances made available by globalization and the Internet are allowing unprecedented collaboration opportunities for the scientific community, from universities and government agencies to small and large corporations. Whether we will continue to make steady progress toward increased collaboration across organizational boundaries, locations, regions, languages, and cultures will depend heavily on an increased ability to manage complexity, ambiguity, risk, and shared ownership; the fostering of more trusting relationships; and developing an appropriate communications infrastructure that helps to connect the brain dots scattered around the globe.

ORGANIZATION OF THE BOOK

This book is divided into three main parts and 12 chapters (see Figure 1–1):

Part I: The Fundamentals
Part II: Making It Happen: The C-Commerce Dimensions
Part III: The Implementation Path

These sections are described as follows.

Part I: The Fundamentals

This section is designed mainly to introduce the reader to the importance of c-commerce. It also introduces our definition of c-commerce and the lenses by which we analyze the many dimensions of collaboration.

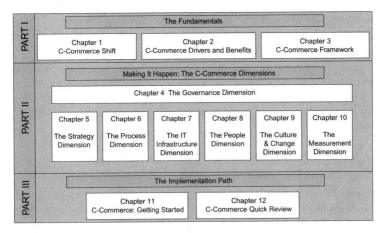

Figure 1–1
Organization of the Book

Chapter 1: C-Commerce Shift
This chapter defines c-commerce and provides an overview of the principal ideas that we explore throughout the book. It provides an overview of the organization of the book and reinforces the imperative of collaborative business strategies.

Chapter 2: C-Commerce Drivers and Benefits
The explicit goal of this chapter is to assemble as many insights and facts as possible to validate that c-commerce is the next competitive advantage. A number of cases are presented to illustrate our points of view and to make the benefits of c-commerce more tangible to the reader.

Chapter 3: C-Commerce Framework
This chapter defines our model for collaboration commerce and introduces ten collaboration capabilities required to clearly help organizations understand c-commerce and develop appropriate collaborative business strategies. These capabilities are lenses that we use to analyze the key dimensions of c-commerce in Part II.

Part II: Making It Happen:
The C-Commerce Dimensions

This section presents the seven dimensions of c-commerce. We explain these dimensions in detail to tackle and embrace c-commerce from a holistic perspective.

Chapter 4: The Governance Dimension
Governance is the number one dimension. If properly addressed, governance will harness the evolution in all other dimensions. It provides the necessary organizational support for the vision around c-commerce. Without leadership understanding to embrace and execute c-commerce, fundamental change will not be realized. In large organizations this can only happen if appropriate governance models are put in place and sponsored by senior management.

Chapter 5: The Strategy Dimension
Strategy in the c-commerce context explores the critical requirement of a clearly defined c-commerce business model and reinforces the explicit goal of including third parties in a broad competitive strategy through global lenses and executed with deep relationship and collaborative frameworks.

Chapter 6: The Process Dimension
A process orientation is a fundamental business step toward c-commerce. Companies that are not organized around processes internally will have a much harder task integrating and collaborating with external parties. This chapter emphasizes the need to develop a clear understanding of mission critical business processes and relationships required to develop and grow in order to maximize business and shareholder value. Ideas, frameworks, and cases are presented to help the reader understand how to improve flows, effectiveness, and execution of business processes.

Chapter 7: The Information Technology
Infrastructure Dimension
In this chapter, we address the building blocks of IT infrastructure that are needed to facilitate and support c-commerce. We also stress the importance of having a distributed IT landscape

that is more open, process-oriented, and integrated. We introduce the idea that IT should be built from the widest perspectives (including key external stakeholders) and strongly argue that companies need to grow their IT infrastructure taking simultaneously into account both their internal needs and the needs of their value chain.

Chapter 8: The People Dimension

This chapter addresses the importance of treating employees as strategic assets and partners of the organization, providing them advanced networking capabilities. It also discusses the major changes that are happening in terms of formal roles and job descriptions. The fact that teams, communities, and projects are increasingly intertwined and need to work seamlessly are thoroughly discussed here.

Chapter 9: The Culture and Change Dimension

The path toward c-commerce should not be opportunistic. Without core values that support and foster c-commerce, most c-commerce initiatives will eventually fail. In this chapter, we discuss some of the key values that should be embraced and disseminated by leaders and organizations moving toward c-commerce.

Chapter 10: The Measurement Dimension

While praising the fast adoption of balanced scorecards, this chapter stresses the importance of including a number of other metrics that reflect an organization's drive and achievements in core processes and in knowledge capabilities. A number of examples of c-commerce metrics are presented in this chapter.

Part III: The Implementation Path

Chapter 11: C-Commerce: Getting Started

This book puts forward a lot of new ideas. Some are grounded on experience and case studies, and others reflect our own vision about how the future will unfold. To instill a clear sense of how to put c-commerce into practice or how to get started, this chapter focuses on helping the reader with some direct and straightforward ways to start implementing c-commerce. We also revisit Chapter 3 and use the capabilities framework to orient the user into an implementation path.

Chapter 12: C-Commerce Quick Review
This chapter provides a quick summary and overview of the book. We think it is a useful chapter both for those who read the whole book and want to recap the key points and for those who want to gain a quick understanding of the topics addressed in the book.

2

C-COMMERCE DRIVERS AND BENEFITS

Awareness of the power of collaboration continues to grow. There are more and more collaborative initiatives—in all walks of life and across areas as diverse as health, community-based human services, cooperative extension programs, social welfare programs, organization knowledge building, leadership, and cooperative business ventures. C-commerce is grounded in the idea that collaboration improves the exchange of information and knowledge while, even more important, it adds value for its diverse stakeholders.

A key driver of c-commerce is the fact that technological advances have made remote collaboration much easier and have greatly reduced transaction costs over the last few years. Phone calls (including long-distance) are close to being completely free in many markets. Internet standards (e.g., XML, SOAP) and Web services are making integration of processes across organizations a viable and less risky option for many organizations. The advent of virtual auctions, online showrooms, secure transactions, and secure communications has allowed the design of online spaces where intellectual property and ideas can be showcased and purchased.

Information and knowledge are spreading globally much more rapidly as individuals are more mobile now than they were a generation ago. A new generation of individuals has been raised with Internet access and an expectation of working and collaborating virtually. The people are already changing notions of allegiance and collaboration.

Companies now need to behave in a coordinated and consistent fashion across the globe, to present a unified image to customers, and to be easily accessible to them. In order to provide customized and personalized products and services, companies will need to provide customers with knowledge of their own operations and try to learn as much as possible about their clients' operations and competitive challenges. Leading organizations can now enable suppliers to directly influence and serve clients' needs. The idea is to let action and decision making happen where expertise and delivery really exist.

In this chapter, we explore in depth a number of the reasons for the growth of collaboration commerce and provide many examples of organizations that are using c-commerce for competitive advantage. A number of reasons are motivating organizations to adopt a c-commerce approach. They are all intertwined. We believe the drivers and benefits of c-commerce can be, however, divided into three key groups:

1. Cost reduction and cycle time reduction
2. Knowledge transfer and learning across the value chain
3. Innovation

We will discuss each of these groups in turn.

COST REDUCTION AND CYCLE TIME REDUCTION

There is an ongoing erosion of vertically integrated supply chains and the rapid emergence of horizontal supply chains. With c-commerce, both resources and management attention can be directed to activities and capabilities that add the greatest value, and the supply chain manager's responsibilities are shifting rapidly from product movement to the integrated supply chain and from customers to suppliers.

These trends allow much higher levels of flexibility in the sourcing of components and in configuring platforms for new product offerings. Real-time supply chain collaboration seeks to respond promptly to customers' requests, whether for additional goods and services or for information. C-commerce can be particularly important to allow quick entry into a new line of business, to enable scaling up to meet seasonal or cyclical demand, and to exploit cross-selling opportunities.

The growth of e-business systems that provide immediate access to up-to-date product catalogs and price lists is reducing the incidence of simple errors. Many e-business systems still give incorrect responses because of the lack of current data from other trading partners. For instance, although an order-processing system may accept an order for goods that are out of stock, this can be avoided by checking all orders against a stock file that is maintained in real time. It may also accept an order for goods that have been reordered from the supplier. To ensure the validity of the customer's order, the order-processing system needs to be able to access the supplier's system.

Billing and Settlement Processes in the U.S. Healthcare Industry

U.S. healthcare providers encounter major delays and waste in their billing and settlement processes. This forms part of the order-to-cash cycle view. Typically, a patient books treatment with a care provider, physician, clinic, or hospital. When the treatment has been completed the care provider bills the patient's "payer" (such as an insurer). It is common for both the patient and the payer to incur fees for the treatment. Payers' rules that define what they will pay for are often complex and are often misunderstood by the patient and the healthcare provider. Such complexity and poor communication create ambiguities and delays. Significant write-offs are common. This should be addressed by building electronic links between care providers and payers. Medical necessity and entitlement can then be assessed before treatment is given and costs are incurred.

As customer tolerance shrinks, a faster response is insufficient. The next generation of value chain collaboration will enable deeper links with key stakeholder trading partners. These links will allow partners to do the following:

- Gain early warning of complex transactions.
- Obtain earlier forecasts to support operational planning.
- Automate fault diagnosis.
- Automate the reordering of supplies with inventory intelligence rules.
- Automate the ease of tracking all service and supply orders to see where the order is in the process and in real time.
- Identify the right knowledge broker contacts in real time as a work-order request moves through the supply chain.
- Enable and support real-time collaborative conversations.
- Overlay business intelligence and analytic capabilities to identify high-value relationships and to deploy adaptive customer service processes for rewarding high-value customers and developing stronger customer retention and acquisition processes.
- Create profiles of all network key stakeholders to support the development of collaborative communities of practice to increase the quality of conversations and knowledge flows.

With these types of deeper linkages into current supply chain work processes, the ability to link separate businesses into value networks, where links are both electronic and commercial, will continue to integrate organizations more tightly. In time, it is conceivable that universal customer and supplier IDs will identify any transaction, interaction, or activity in the extended value chain.

As collaborative business models built from work process and relationship networks become deeper and more pervasive, the origins of a transaction will become more difficult to trace. They will interact more like dynamic network intelligent nodes rather than individual transaction nodes. This transformation will require new sophisticated levels of risk management systems to simultaneously monitor and measure intangible assets in all directions.

Links with trading partners can provide direct operational benefits. Electronic links will mean that error rates are lower, orders are less likely to include obsolete prices or product codes, and ambiguities can be removed sooner and off the critical path, reducing delay.

Traditionally, each function or business area develops its own forecast based on history or general trend information supplied by key customers. In contrast, c-commerce requires the sharing of forecast information with the appropriate supply chain partners and process owners. Uncertainty is reduced and better forecasting information is available, lessening the need for excessive buffer inventory.

Companies such as IBM are offering advanced customer relationship management (CRM) software solutions and initiatives such as CPFR (collaborative planning, forecasting, and replenishment) that are changing the relationship between trading partners. CPFR defines a business process model for supply chain partners to coordinate plans and reduce variance between supply and demand, which results in higher service levels, higher in-stock performance, and lower inventories. The critical elements are relationship networks and governance models that are enabled through collaboration at all levels in the system and are designed to learn in real time from multiple exchanges.

Cisco and FedEx

Cisco Systems' ambition to close its books on a daily basis gave rise to the company's real-time enterprise solution. Consider the benefits of having all information current in all systems so books can be nominally closed within hours of the end of a quarter (or day). Cisco does this now and, after adjustments that include managerial and auditor input, the company can announce financial results within 3 days of the end of the quarter. Cisco's much vaunted electronic order-entry system has decreased the company's error rate from 20% to 0.2% and by as much as 8% to 10% for after-sales service.

> FedEx could not economically provide the level of cus-
> tomer service that it delivers without sophisticated infor-
> mation technology systems. The costs to FedEx of a
> package-pickup call or a "where is my package?" inquiry
> have declined substantially (to 10% of earlier costs)
> because of the use of appropriate real-time technology
> solutions.

KNOWLEDGE TRANSFER AND LEARNING ACROSS THE VALUE CHAIN

The potential benefits of c-commerce capabilities are consider-
able and measurable. Competitive wars continue to improve and
optimize value chains by gaining more competitive intelligence at
key knowledge or transaction flow points. Leading organizations
have clearly understood that developing deliberate mechanisms
for transferring knowledge up and down the value chain is critical to shared success. Perhaps no other company exemplifies this
better than Toyota. The company's ability to maintain strong relationships with its suppliers is one of the key reasons for its leadership in the auto industry. Many have tried to imitate it (even
with more modern e-hubs), but still no other auto manufacturer
has been able to show the same level of commitment to its suppliers. A recent study by professors Jeffrey H. Dyer and Nile W.
Hatch (2004) has shown that this level of commitment is still
unmatched and that the results are very tangible:

- Toyota knowledge-sharing schemes with its suppliers have
  cost the organization between $50 million and $100
  million in the United States and Japan over the last 35
  years. Toyota sent personnel to visit U.S. suppliers' plants
  to exchange technical information an average of 13 days
  each year—twice the rate of competitors.
- By 1996 Toyota suppliers had achieved 10% higher output
  per worker, 25% lower inventories, and 50% fewer defects
  in their manufacturing cells in comparison to what had
  been achieved for their largest U.S. customer (one of the
  Big Three automakers).
- The price premium of Toyota vehicles over U.S. cars in the
  same class is around 10% for new cars and 18% for used

ones. A major reason for this is higher quality: Studies have found that between 1990 and 2000, Toyota cars had roughly 40% fewer problems (per 100 vehicles) than other major U.S. auto manufacturers.

In the early stages of a knowledge-sharing network, Toyota establishes itself at the center of a hub of bilateral relationships with suppliers. Suppliers strongly identify with the network and feel obliged to share knowledge more freely with other members. They begin to form ties with each other in nested subnetworks, and these multilateral relationships help initiate and better route knowledge flows. Multiple pathways then exist for transferring both explicit and tacit knowledge and, in a mature network, the amount of tacit knowledge being transferred is substantial. Toyota has developed interorganizational processes that facilitate the transfer of both explicit and tacit knowledge within its supplier network; these consist of three key processes: supplier associations, consulting/problem-solving groups, and voluntary learning teams (see related case study).

Toyota's Interorganizational Processes for Knowledge Transfer

SUPPLIER ASSOCIATIONS

Supplier associations have been the vehicle through which links to suppliers were established and explicit knowledge has been transferred—including Toyota policies and widely applicable best practices. Regular meetings of supplier associations—the Bluegrass Automotive Manufacturers Association (BAMA) in the United States and *kyohokai* in Japan—provide a forum for sharing valuable knowledge. They enable high-level sharing of explicit strategic knowledge regarding production plans, policies, market trends, and implications for the supply network. They also allow more frequent interactions around cost, quality, safety, and social activities. The associations often set medium-term objectives—such as to eliminate supplier design defects—and they also help to develop relationships among the participating suppliers.

CONSULTING/PROBLEM-SOLVING GROUPS

Consultants offer intensive on-site assistance from experts in Toyota processes as well as workshops and seminars. Personal visits from consultants have been effective in transferring high-value tacit knowledge and in fostering an atmosphere of reciprocity among suppliers. Knowledge sharing has enabled them to make significant improvements to their operations both in Japan and in the United States:

- *In Japan:* The operations management consulting division (OMCD) has acquired, stored, and diffused valuable production knowledge residing within the Toyota Group since the mid-1960s. The OMCD is led by six highly experienced senior executives; each of them has responsibility for two Toyota plants and approximately 10 suppliers. The division includes about 30 senior consultants and sometimes 20 junior consultants who are rotated. Members of the Toyota Group are not charged for consultants' time and suppliers in Japan have received an average of 4.2 visits per year, each lasting 3.1 days.
- *In the United States:* Toyota Supplier Support Center (now TSSC, Inc.) was started in 1992 and now has about 20 consultants engaged in knowledge-transfer processes. It requires participating Toyota suppliers to share their project results with others, allowing "best practice" suppliers to be highlighted and encouraging suppliers to open their operations to one another to allow cross-learning and replication. Some areas can remain off-limits to visitors to protect companies' proprietary knowledge.

VOLUNTARY LEARNING TEAMS

Learning-team strategy involves on-site sharing of know-how within small teams of 6 to 12 suppliers to strengthen multilateral ties between suppliers and facilitate the sharing of tacit knowledge among them. In Japan, *jishuken* study groups are an advanced knowledge-sharing mechanism to explore new ideas. They transfer the lessons learned to Toyota and throughout the supplier network. In 1994, the concept was extended to the United States and three plant development activities (PDA) core groups were set up among 40 suppliers and with voluntary membership. A key reason that group visits by PDAs and transfers of tacit knowledge have been particularly effective is that they involve learning that is context-specific.

Source: Dyer & Hatch 2004

INNOVATION

Globalization has increased the need for the rapid creation, diffusion, and adaptation of new innovations. In many industries it is no longer possible to innovate with a focus on a single market. Other markets cannot be an afterthought. The innovation process (particularly disruptive innovation) increasingly requires a combination of different skills, technologies, and disciplines. As business operations and planning become more integrated, companies are under intense pressure to deliver innovative products to market as quickly and cost effectively as possible. There is a strong need to actively engage all participants in the product lifecycle by maximizing their ability to collaborate.

Another aspect that is worth highlighting is the fact that many firms are uncovering, and realizing value from, the hidden gems of intellectual property that they have developed over time (e.g., software, methods, patents) and are unable to exploit alone and in a timely fashion. In certain industries (e.g., electronics) it is becoming quite impossible to innovate without infringing other companies' patents. This scenario has led many organizations to seek joint developments and/or broad cross-licensing of their portfolio of patents.

In fact, in many cases there is strong interdependence among the ongoing evolution of research and development (R&D) efforts of different players in the same value chain. This requires the co-evolution of R&D efforts. There is the possibility for developing joint intellectual property (IP) or the development of IP clearinghouses that provide access to the IP of other businesses while maintaining separate IP rights for each company.

Other trends that are worth mentioning include the following:

- R&D can be outsourced with the emergence of organizations that are dedicated to developing new ideas and inventing new products (skunk works for hire) (Schwarz 2004).
- The rapid growth in the number of technology-based companies' incubators and lower capital needs in some fields provide interesting opportunities for entrepreneurs in knowledge-based industries.
- The open-source approach to software development that has migrated to other fields (e.g., medicine).
- The consolidation of online intellectual property markets (see related case study).

Emergence of Intellectual Property (IP) Markets

IP virtual market spaces are entering a consolidation phase, and three models of market spaces have taken hold:

- All-in-one service. Generally includes a contacts database, a matching service for seekers and providers, submission of requests for quotes, and project and payment process. NineSigma and CanBioTech are good examples.
- Shop window or auction. This model openly displays technology wants and needs according to the areas where expertise is sought. The range of sites varies from highly speculative, such as NewIdeaTrade.com, to more specific, such as yet2.com, an Internet "dating service" for IP users and providers. Finally, there are sites with an extremely tight industry focus, such as Pharmalicensing.com and 2RentACoder.com,

which currently has more than 80,000 registered programmers in its database with an environment similar to eBay but exclusively for software development contract work.

- Reward or challenge. These are usually biotechnology and pure science sites that offer a bounty for those who solve a problem or challenge posted on the site in exchange for the intellectual property rights of the innovation. InnoCentive.com is a market leader and is underwritten by Eli Lilly with the strong participation of Procter & Gamble, Dow, and BASF.

Some of the ideas that initially pushed Eli Lilly (an $11 billion company, with an annual $2 billion R&D budget) to invest in InnoCentive were nicely summarized by its chief information officer, W. Roy Dunbar (CIO *Insight* 2002): "We're very clever within Lilly in (our) Indianapolis headquarters, but we also recognize there are a lot of other clever folk in other places. There are communities of world-class chemists in the states of the former Soviet Union, in India, and in China. InnoCentive is an attempt to explore how to access those communities via a Web site that posts specific problems in chemistry and a financial bounty for the first viable solution."

Large multinationals are rapidly moving away from "ivory tower" R&D centers. In order to reduce labor costs and find innovative local solutions, these multinationals have shifted to developing centers of competence spread in many developed countries and increasingly also in developing countries. The case of Dell Computer Corp. is quite illustrative. Most of its software (for internal use) is now being developed in Brazil, Russia, and India. Data show that a number of large organizations are already decentralizing R&D (especially smaller developed countries such as Sweden, the Netherlands, and Switzerland). Figures show a ready basis for extending international research participation, partnerships, and collaboration (Rycroft 2002):

- European firms have the highest proportion of R&D abroad (about 30%)—much of it in other European countries.
- About 10% to 12% of American R&D and about 10% of Japanese R&D has been internationalized.
- About 15% of patents granted in the United States are generated by foreign subsidiaries of multinational companies (MNCs).
- The share of patents generated by foreign MNC subsidiaries in Europe is about 30%.
- The most internationalized patenting takes place in older manufacturing sectors such as food and paper products, while the least internationalization is in more complex sectors such as semiconductors.
- U.S. patent filings from foreign entities were expected to surpass those from U.S. entities for the first time in 2004 (Schwarz 2004).
- In countries such as Canada and the United Kingdom, foreign-funded R&D accounts for nearly 25% of total industrial R&D (National Science Board, Science and Engineering Indicators 2004).
- R&D performed by American companies abroad jumped from $4.6 billion in 1986 to about $20 billion in 2000 (U.S. Department of Commerce 2003).
- Interesting corporate examples include the following:
  - Procter & Gamble, which has 40% of its 8,000 research staff outside North America (Knopman 2003)
  - Nokia, which has 18,000 engineers doing R&D work spread across 69 sites from Boston to Bangalore (Kaihla 2002)
  - UTStarcom, which has more than 1,400 engineers in China and 150 engineers in India (CFO *Magazine* 2003)
  - Alcatel, the French giant, which raised its R&D investment in Shanghai to $100 million for work on third-generation mobile infrastructure and applications (CFO *Magazine* 2003)
  - AstraZeneca, a leading British firm, which is rapidly increasing its investments in R&D in India (CFO *Magazine* 2003)
  - E.piphany (a $100 million California-based software company), which is outsourcing 30% to 40% of its engineers in China (CFO *Magazine* 2003)

Perhaps the most impressive evidence of the importance of collaboration is data provided by the U.S. Department of Commerce. It shows that between 1991 and 2001, U.S. companies participated in more than 4,600 research and technology alliances involving foreign countries. These alliances were particularly strong in the IT and biotechnology industries, confirming that the fast-moving industries are those that demand more collaboration and sharing of risks. The data also show that contracting R&D has been increasing steadily over the last 15 years. By 2001, it already accounted for 11.7% of R&D spending in the chemicals manufacturing industry and 18.7% in the pharmaceuticals manufacturing industry (from about 8% in 1990).

The pharmaceutical industry offers further compelling evidence of the need for collaboration. Not too long ago, the senior vice president for research and development for Pfizer, Dr. John Niblack, pointed out: "We are also extending our reach beyond our corporate walls, to establish relationships with dozens of small organizations on the leading edge of research in such areas as viruses, bacteria and certain genes. As big and talented as our corporate research team is, today's fast-paced advances are too diverse and dynamic for any one organization to handle alone" (Kanter 1997).

By accessing expertise from a variety of stakeholders, companies can extend their products and services in new ways. The trend of banding together to share R&D costs and address regulatory requirements—like greenhouse emissions—on a truly global scale is very evident in the oil, chemical, and automotive industries. These alliances prove that, year on year, the practice of combining their powerful networks to work strategically and collaboratively has been able to influence industry outcomes.

Collaboration in the Aerospace and Copier Market Industries

The aerospace industry offers a number of interesting examples of collaboration in product development.

The dispute between Brazil's Embraer and Canada's Bombardier

Embraer was almost bankrupt in the mid-1990s, yet it made the unlikely comeback to become the third-largest commercial aircraft manufacturer in the world, surpassing Bombardier. How did this happen? How did a company from a developing country, competing in a high-tech market, beat a once superior, profitable, and domineering competitor in less than a decade? There are a number of ingredients that contributed to the company's success, but one is fundamental: Embraer's relative lack of funding and technical resources led the company to embrace a much more collaborative product development process than Bombardier. Embraer developed partnerships with American, French, German, and Brazilian universities and with small and large organizations from South America, the United States, Japan, and Europe. These included Piper Aircraft Company, United Technologies, Northrop, McDonnell Douglas, Parker Hannifin (United States); Aermacchi, Microtecnica, Latecoere (Italy); Kawasaki (Japan); Liebherr (Germany); Gamesa Group (Spain); Sonaca (Belgium); and Enaer (Chile). The company headquarters came to resemble a veritable United Nations, with suppliers and partners from different continents speaking different languages engaged in rapid product development projects through risk-sharing contracts. Indeed, Embraer became very similar to some of the finest Japanese auto producers that, through a system called *keiretsu,* engage suppliers, partners, and clients in very open, trusting, and shared destiny commitments.

Most recently, Embraer has shown how innovation, talent, and collaboration have no limits. In great need of young talent to build and work on new products, and realizing that there wasn't enough of a supply of qualified aeronautics engineers in Brazil, the company set up a very innovative in-house master's program in aeronautics to attract the best to work for them. In order to establish the program, the company carefully studied every engineering and related discipline program in Brazilian universities. Then, it convinced different universities and departments to team up with Embraer's own Ph.D.'s to develop a unique program to attend to the company's most pressing needs. Young scientists and engineers who participate in this program are paid to earn a master's degree. The result is that a new batch of scientists and engineers is produced each year and they are already helping Embraer to develop new generations of planes.

The development of the joint strike fighter and the 777 by Boeing

The joint strike fighter (JSF) was developed by only 58 of Boeing's employees, who coordinated the hundreds of suppliers that developed most of the plane's modules. In the case of the 777 aircraft, 238 cross-functional teams and a large number of suppliers and customers engaged in a very collaborative environment to develop the plane with 50% fewer change requests, errors, and rework than previous plane development projects that did not incorporate collaboration as a core element of doing work. In both cases, the collaborative efforts were greatly assisted by the use of advanced digital collaboration and shared computerized modeling tools. In developing the 777, the innovative use of computing technology led the company to win the top spot in the manufacturing category of the annual Computerworld Smithsonian Awards.

Copiers: Open Innovation at Océ

From the Netherlands comes the interesting case of Océ. Océ is a leading Dutch company with 18,000 employees (1,500 in R&D); it is a key competitor to Canon and Xerox in the high-end copier market. According to Professor Roel Rutten, who did a comprehensive study of the innovation process at Océ, the company made the major change from having a closed R&D environment to a system of open innovation (Rutten 2003):

"In the early 1990s, the main purpose of the fence around the site of Océ R&D in Venlo, the Netherlands, was to prevent knowledge from leaking out. Today, some 250 people from universities, engineering bureaus, software developers, and suppliers work side by side with Océ engineers inside that fence" (Rutten 2003). He goes on to say: "The fundamental R&D is often done on a global scale, using the knowledge and expertise of leading institutes and universities. Whether these institutes are located in Japan, the United States, or the Netherlands is irrelevant. What matters is that Océ acquires the knowledge it needs" (Rutten 2003).

Sources: Quinn 2000, Boeing.com

Evidence suggests that new innovations and technologies can arise from anywhere in the world and are more likely to arise from collaboration (internal and external) than from individual work. It is also increasingly common for cutting-edge technologies to be developed by a number of different institutions, combining the skills of small and large, private and public organizations. Innovation in isolation is no longer a viable option.

Recent research studies (Booze-Allen 2004, Christensen 2004, Keeley 2004, Gordon 2004) have found that innovation is the engine powering long-term value. In Keeley's recent research of thousands of companies from around the world (2004), he has empirically shown that one of the most significant drivers of innovation is the quality of networks and their collaborative strength. Booze-Allen's (2004) research indicates that organizations dramatically improve their revenues and profitability— sometimes by a multiplier of ten—when they focus on product and customer service innovation practices. However, when you peel back the layers of these research models, you consistently find that the quality of the collaborative conversations and collaborative relationships is the glue that enables the exchange of new ideas.

Conclusion

Enterprises that embrace c-commerce can expect streamlined business processes, new cost efficiencies, greater customer satisfaction and loyalty, and greatly expanded revenue potential. Although each member of the collaborative community continues to perform a specific set of tasks and functions, the sharing of information and knowledge achieved through c-commerce will result in significant competitive advantages for all concerned.

The greatest risk today is being timid. Many companies recycle the litany of excuses for not embracing c-commerce and choose to ignore the prevailing tide of business networking and globalization. Not enough companies make a positive decision to implement c-commerce as a strategic initiative to continuously improve their core work processes and to effectively adapt to marketplace and customer changes. In fact, they may be motivated by dissatisfaction with the results in a given process and make an emotional decision to implement c-commerce as the solution for performance inadequacies, without even understanding the causes of the problems or evaluating alternatives.

Someone in the executive suite, usually the chief executive or another executive vice president, may come to the conclusion that c-commerce will improve cycle time within processes and therefore reduce cost. They may even dispatch a team of people to look at a variety of options, but the outcome would lean toward selecting the process-focused c-commerce option. Because the idea to implement c-commerce comes from the top of the organization, it can have a momentum that is hard to counter.

C-commerce is a realistic and compelling business option that merits wide support and a careful, balanced evaluation. Progressive and ambitious companies are mastering the art of integrating c-commerce into their business models. In this way, they are focusing their resources where value is greatest and where growth is most promising. We believe that the arguments and cases presented in this chapter about cost reduction, learning, and innovation derived from c-commerce are very convincing. Business leaders should pay close attention to similar events, trends, and cases in their own industries. Using the perspectives provided in this book, they are bound to find examples of c-commerce everywhere they look. If they have not yet started along their own paths toward c-commerce, they are already late in the game.

3

C-COMMERCE
FRAMEWORK

There is increasing leadership understanding that business dynamics, new business models, and supply chain relationships are complex ecosystems requiring real-time and collaborative infrastructure(s) to compete effectively. Changing market dynamics create new executive realities that firms in both private and public sectors have to evaluate and create new solutions for to be more effective over time. Leaders want the fundamentals and not the latest "management fad." We all know that the world changes and continues to change at an accelerated pace, and if the way we are looking at the firm is not providing new insights, then we need a new filter to look through. What we are introducing here is not a new management idea but a fundamental approach to tapping into people, understanding how and why they communicate, what drivers and cultural context motivates them to share their knowledge, and what relationship networks are accessible and reachable to help answer some of the most complex problems leaders face. The c-commerce value proposition is to improve the ability to embrace innovation and change more rapidly and sustain effective operating practices and business strategies while preserving what is core. Much of what is broken in our organizations has come about because leaders have not recognized the fundamental shifts in consumer power, technology reach, and knowledge-worker needs.

Alan Greenspan, chairman of the U.S. Federal Reserve, characterized the "collaborative economy" in this observation: "America's economic output, measured in tons, is barely any heavier than it was 100 years ago, but the GDP has increased twentyfold. In such an economy, value, and wealth, is created primarily from the specialized knowledge of individuals and communities. The ability to effectively cultivate, share, and use knowledge collaboratively is now a primary source of competitive momentum." AMR Research analyst Bob Parker, an expert on business-to-business activities, sees that the concept of collaboration has significant value. He views it as a major component of a larger next generation of e-business infrastructure that supports not only an individual firm, but also its customers and trading partners (2004). By 2007, the need for real-time business processes and measurement will drive the Global 1000 companies to redeploy next generation real-time processing infrastructure solutions that are collaborative in design (Gartner Group 2004). The market for knowledge management (KM) software reached U.S. $5.4 billion by 2004. The service market for KM services will increase from $11 billion in 2004 to $20 billion in 2010 (IDC).

DEFINING C-COMMERCE

The origins of collaboration commerce—"c-commerce"—are derived from how collaboration improves information and knowledge exchange, adding value to its diverse stakeholders. C-commerce involves taking advantage of collaboration best practices, business dynamics, and relationship networks to change the way the firm works internally and externally. By sharing business processes and leveraging knowledge through people and collaborative solutions, c-commerce allows for greater cooperation among business partners and provides greater value to customers. Collaborative organizations are flexible and fluid, and they avoid restrictive, tightly coupled, and static business relationships. Instead they use more dynamic, loosely joined, and opportunistic approaches focused on synchronization.

Organizations that embrace c-commerce are rapidly delivering results from more streamlined business processes, new cost efficiencies, greater customer satisfaction and loyalty, human capital productivity, and exponential revenue growth. Successful collaboration efforts by organizations include the following: minimizing duplication of efforts and services; a long-term orientation for safeguards; a clear mission that will evolve over time; mobilization of resources through diverse abilities and approaches; power in numbers; and improvements in trust and communication among customers, competitors, and employees.

C-COMMERCE CAPABILITIES

One of the major challenges for any leader is making sense of the new language being used in next generation business models like c-commerce. For example, in a virtual world, *place* is no longer defined by bricks and mortar; place can be largely virtual as more and more business is conducted virtually. C-commerce consists of ten major capabilities required to design, develop, and execute a successful c-commerce business transformation. The c-commerce capabilities are outlined in this chapter in detail and include the following:

1. Purpose
2. Identity
3. Reputation
4. Trust
5. Commerce
6. Transparency
7. Networks
8. Boundaries
9. Real-time collaboration enterprise (RTCE)
10. Governance

Purpose—The Driver

Successful collaboration, business dynamics, and networks are all built from a shared purpose. If the purpose is well defined and agreed on by individuals, firms, and partners throughout the value chain, then interactions function effectively and achieving desired results is possible. Relationships develop when there is a mutual desire or jointly perceived need to connect and generate an action. People need a purpose and then a reason to collaborate. This shared interest or goal built from a common purpose will become the center or core to initiate an exchange. Establishing the reason for the collaborative interaction is a critical and usually a conscious step. These initial conversations become the "trust-making" foundation of relationships and partnerships.

Once a relationship has started to form, leaders must make certain that the central purpose of the ongoing exchanges and interactions is implicitly shared by all members involved. There is little point in establishing a network where individual members are all pursuing disparate aims. The goals and business strategies may well change and evolve over the course of time; an ongoing and open dialogue should be fostered to maintain focus and develop further relationships. The purpose of relationships, firms, and partnerships is a dynamic learning journey. Purposeful, authentic, and engaging conversations are the roots that inspire change. Purpose is how each of our lives will make the world a better place to live for the next generation. In a survey of 230 personnel executives, the American Society of Training and Development found that teams with an understood core purpose were able to accomplish a substantial rise in performance in key areas. These included productivity, quality of production, job satisfaction, reduction in time wasted, and customer satisfaction. At 3M, for example, the core purpose is to solve unsolved problems innovatively. The core purpose of Israel is to provide a secure place on Earth for the Jewish people. Theaters were originally established for the core purpose of providing a place for people to flourish and enhancing the community.

There is no limit to the potential of a good relationship established with a shared purpose. Given an "impossible" task, members will reinforce each other's confidence as they seek to turn the impossible into reality. The collective ability to innovate is stronger because they agree on what they are trying to accomplish. Even small numbers of individuals, firms, and partners working together will exceed the accomplishments of any one individual working alone. By establishing and agreeing on the group's purpose and shared objectives, its members will go beyond simple, useful improvements and achieve significant breakthroughs. For example, several engineers were pulled together and asked to significantly improve the reliability of a specific machine. Several team members, when first brought together, thought the objective was unattainable. Working together with a clear definition of what they had come together to accomplish, however, they were able to produce and execute a plan that tripled performance of the machine.

Identity—The Persona Kaleidoscope

People have many identities or personas. There are personal profiles that identify aspects of who we are, what we need, what we do, and what we like. Personal profiles are compiled from statistics, surveys, and categories into which each of us is grouped. A single individual is a complex matrix of attributes. The unlimited combinations of these attributes create our digital personas. There are aspects of leadership, parenting techniques and family dynamics, job responsibilities and performance, competencies and certifications, community involvement, and vacation and entertainment activities. As our lives unfold, the elements and aspects of our personas change and grow. In addition, the complexity and effectiveness of our personal profiles will continue to drive and affect future marketing programs.

Some of the literature emerging (Allen 2004) defines persona as character type. Character is an important quality of an individual's persona because it defines relationship attributes that determine relevance, but it also affects the confidence and trust dynamics of any collaborative relationship. Character relates to the following attributes: leadership style, integrity, clarity of motives for collaborating, consistency of behavior, openness, trustworthiness, and discretion.

No two people are exactly alike. By looking at personal profiles from multiple perspectives, our lives become the roles we perform. These can include coordinator, ideas person, critic, external contact, implementer, leader, and teacher. It is useful to bear these roles in mind when considering candidates for virtual teams, implementing change, and building partnerships and relationships. Never forget that the most important function of an individual, firm, or supply chain is to understand a shared purpose and achieve the defined objectives. Try to match roles to personality based on individual profiles. It is not necessary for each person to perform only one function. The linkages between purpose, identity, and reputation create a powerful new form of competitive intelligence. For example, leaders find and develop individuals, continuously improve business dynamics and exchanges, and leverage networks to meet defined goals and objectives. The characteristics to look for in personal profiles include the following: excellent judge of the talents and personalities of individuals, adept at finding ways of overcoming weaknesses, excellent communication skills, and skilled at inspiring and sustaining enthusiasm.

Reputation—Character and Image

Reputation is about character. It has been said that the best evidence of a man's reputation is his whole life. Just like a person, the reputation of an organization or industry is a reflection over time, as seen through the eyes of its stakeholders—customers, investors, employees, and the media—who consider such factors as product quality, management, financial performance, social responsibility, and market leadership. Therefore, a reputation is built and earned over time and cannot be bought.

Reputation is more visible and important than ever before. Millions of people participating in online public discussion groups have made the Internet the people's forum, where everyone contributes and every opinion counts, and where news—good or bad, rumor or fact—travels faster than by any other medium. A single unhappy customer, misinformed consumer, or disgruntled employee can spark an online and offline reputation disaster for the firm. It is important to use relationships, partnerships, and networks to identify and defuse potential reputation disasters for the firm before they become "breaking news."

A positive corporate reputation can be crucial to future growth and the development of a c-commerce firm. Consider the reputation of the firm from four specific viewpoints: (1) dynamic exploitation of existing assets, (2) development of core competencies, (3) image management, and (4) strategic alliances. There are a variety of differing policies and practices used by countries, industries, and firms to improve an existing reputation or establish a good reputation. Reputation is complex and is an interdependency of assets, core competencies, image, and strategic alliances that cannot be separated from each other. Rather than focus on one aspect of reputation, invest in a broad spectrum of reputation-building views to quickly develop an image for excellence in the appropriate industry and marketplace. Positive reputations often depend on the extent to which firms develop an integrated package of policies and solutions for leaders, partners, and relationship networks to quickly take advantage of when they need them. These policies and solutions allow people to quickly connect and collaborate with resources throughout the relationship network to continuously improve reputations over time and defuse reputation disasters when they occur.

Trust—The Core Value

Core values are the firm's essential and enduring convictions. They are guiding principles and are usually thought to provide competitive advantage for the firm, but that is not why people, firms, and networks implement them. We have core values because they define what is important to us and frame how we work or how we make decisions. Every firm will decide what values need to be core. It is important that the firm has core values. Maybe trust is on the list of core values and maybe it is not. To successfully implement c-commerce, trust needs to be a core value or a dimension of existing practices or strategies within the firm. It is fundamental to building and sustaining an effective relationship network.

For effective collaboration processes, trust is the core value establishing the balance among strategy, people, process, and systems in designing a "collaboratively intelligent" organization. Many recent global surveys that monitor top executive and employee or consumer attitudes continue to find that there is a trust crisis with boards, chief executives, their leadership teams, and unions. A recent review by a consumer publication stated that "more than two thirds of the jobs in the United States economy depend upon consumer expenditure." However, few consumers, employees, investors, or shareholders trust their service providers. According to one recent U.S. survey, 96% of consumers say they do not trust their health maintenance organization, 93% do not trust their health insurance providers, and 88% do not trust their telecom providers. Only 60% of the population mistrusts their supermarket (the highest rating).

Trust is the ultimate motivator and is gained through experience. When expectations are well defined and individuals deliver what they have communicated or promised, the depth of trust increases. Trust and time are deeply linked: Trust increases based on the number of positive interactions over time. When trusted relationships develop over time, the value of an enterprise's social and c-commerce networks increases. Cultivating environments where trust prevails is critical as major decisions are made by some form of group decision, rather than by one person. If trust among group members is eliminated, a vital component of group cohesion—the force that holds the group together—is dissolved. People are fairly predictable; they will not work for very long for, let alone support enthusiastically, anyone whose motives they doubt. People are engaged and will cooperate openly with individuals they trust. More importantly, people transfer their knowledge willingly to others they trust, improving innovation and growth in firms.

Commerce—The Knowledge Flow

Commerce in collaboration is about sharing and exchanging information to create knowledge. The ability to focus on the primary delivery methods will produce the most effective results. Because knowledge flow is the exchange of information and the levers are the primary delivery methods, we combined the two to create knowledge flow exchange levers. There are three major knowledge flow exchange levers to consider: (1) reciprocity, (2) dynamic real-time exchange, and (3) the quality of conversations.

Reciprocity
Reciprocity is the back-and-forth or give-and-take that occurs in conversations and relationships. Based on purpose, identity, reputation, and trust, these conversations are the foundation for relationship capital within the firm and across the supply chain. Use expertise-locating and social-networking technology, combined with communities of practice competencies, to actively cultivate reciprocity or "structural ties" to improve knowledge flows in the firm, partnerships, and relationship networks.

Benjamin Franklin said, "Always ask people for favors. People will ask you to return them. That is how one painstakingly constructs a free exchange, which is the basis of all public and private business—one polite request at a time." Reciprocity is built on a foundation of frequent and relevant collaborative exchanges to teach and learn from each other.

Dynamic Real-Time Exchange

Dynamic real-time exchange is about timing. The objective is to deliver information in a timely matter to the firm, partnerships, and relationship networks. Team members' ability to quickly find people and share information is essential to improve productivity, production quality, job satisfaction, and customer satisfaction and reduce time wasted. There are a variety of ways this can be accomplished. Users will need to share a common set of collaboration, content management, and knowledge management technologies to support publishing information, improving search results, empowering global virtual teams, and quickly connecting with each other. Moving forward, leaders should consider investments and continuous improvement in collaborative technologies and tools that support cross-functional work teams to improve their real-time productivity.

The Quality of Conversations

Thoughtful conversations are the primary source of organizational intelligence. Knowledge creation is primarily a social rather than an individual process. People learn together in conversation as they work and practice together. The speed of collaborative interchanges will continue to evolve as firms strive to innovate more rapidly. Leaders cannot underestimate the value of creating and fostering corporate cultures that recognize and support conversation as a core business process and a source of competitive advantage. SAS Airlines in Stockholm has created a central plaza in the middle of its corporate headquarters with shops and cafes where individuals from all levels and functions throughout the firm are encouraged to visit and share ideas to grow as a community. Dow Chemical has set up innovative work spaces where employees can collaborate in open modern spaces. Starbucks, one of the most rapidly growing companies, refers to employees as partners, and all partner meetings are forums of conversations where each partner is treated with respect and dignity; such trust-building rituals are among the factors that contribute to the company's incredible success.

Transparency—Informed and Committed Stakeholders

Transparency is about communicating clearly. For c-commerce to succeed, it is vital that everyone who needs information is informed and can easily access needed details. All stakeholders need to be identified and communicated with so they understand what the process or strategy will do for them and their commitment will be confirmed. Because stakeholders have a vested interest in the business process or strategic plan, they each need to be kept informed of developments relevant to them. Keep the language simple and define all important terms: Remember that even a word such as *cost* can have different meanings to different people within the same organization.

Transparency is about getting feedback. Make sure there is a feedback mechanism in place for stakeholders to share what they think of the process or plan and its impact on them. Everyone in the firm should be viewed as the eyes and ears of the team. The sales people, for example, know what customers are saying, and process owners have an insider's view of how work gets done. Each has a role to play in checking and molding c-commerce. Make sure communication channels are open, relationships are established, and everyone is listening. Then listen some more. Feedback, when done effectively, will spark changes and improvement to business processes and strategic plans.

Disclosure legislation trends driven by Sarbanes-Oxley, the American Health Insurance Portability and Accountability Act, and Basel II are making firms focus on stakeholder identification. Throughout the firm and supply chain we are asking, "So what does this mean to me and the way I do my job?" Spend more time identifying the right stakeholders. They might be internal or external to the firm. Begin to gain commitment to the roles stakeholders play in business processes and strategic plans, and understand when it is important to confirm these commitments in writing. Communicating the results of business processes and strategic plans is a continuous process. Ensure that every process owner and strategy owner is regularly updating progress to identified stakeholders. New forms of mass communication and interactive teleconferences are helping to encourage increased transparency. Developing management and operating know-how around what transparency fundamentally means will heighten awareness that each communication is a recording. Ensure exchanges are memorable and add value for c-commerce to accelerate.

Networks—The Social Nexus

Today we live in a world of networks. From networks of suppliers to networks of computers and from networks of trading partners to networks of activists, the world is linked and taking advantage of these connections. Each instant there are tens of thousands of new network links made through the Internet, between cell phones, Web sites, business-to-business exchanges, and online communities. These links create a social nexus that provides individuals, customers, and firms with information, insight, and opportunities.

A well-developed social nexus or relationship network enables transparency within the firm. The identification of stakeholders becomes less complicated as the relationship network provides a new depth of knowledge around who needs to know what and then provides the reciprocity to provide the quick updates and information exchange needed. The grapevine is a social nexus that already exists in the firm. We want to formalize and improve on the corporate grapevine to establish the firm's relationship network. There are four areas to focus on: (1) reciprocity—determine the strength of relationships throughout the network and the type of knowledge being exchanged, (2) dynamic real-time exchange—evaluate the time frame, frequency, and knowledge sharing of relationships, (3) the quality of conversations—establish how effective the exchange of information is throughout the relationship network, and (4) health—identify how relationships are continuously improving and meeting identified c-commerce objectives.

Some companies have programs in place to ensure that key stakeholder feedback is implemented through the social nexus as part of innovation processes. A recent example is Novo Nordisk, a pharmaceutical company based in Denmark. To better fight diabetes, the company has established an ongoing dialogue with patients, as well as networks of doctors and nurses. By accessing expertise from a variety of stakeholders, firms can extend their products and services in new ways. The trend toward banding together to share research and development costs and address regulatory requirements such as greenhouse emissions on a global scale is very evident in the oil, chemical, and automotive industries. The result is that year-on-year, by combining their powerful ecosystems, the collective partnerships are able to strategically and collaboratively influence industry outcomes.

Boundaries—The Rules

Boundaries create fixed points and establish the guidelines we work within. An important c-commerce boundary involves privacy and permission. It is hard to think of a time when we are not being watched by one system or another. Software monitors our keystrokes, and cameras, hidden or otherwise, are everywhere. This can be looked at as the downside of living in an electronic world. On the other hand, there are benefits to capturing all this information and passing it among individuals, partners, relationship networks, and supply chains. Consider open systems and new collaboration systems developed and driven by personal profiles and permission-based exchange models. These systems will continue to improve. It is becoming less and less complicated to connect people to people, content to content, and people to content.

Another boundary is physical space and place. As the world becomes increasingly interconnected, the use of new collaboration-support online tools, such as webinars, and teleconferencing are becoming more common. More diverse teams are being formed to work on projects and support and improve global business processes. Virtual tools and physical space are being combined to manage the quality of relationships, develop stronger trust, and ensure there is a balance between face-to-face and computer-mediated interactions.

Boundaries are shifting. The ability to differentiate between short- and long-term thinking and strike a balance between the two is an integral part of implementing business processes and developing strategic plans. Short-term planning deals with the here and now, and long-term thinking looks further into the future. If the firm's boundaries are focused entirely on the current enterprise, then expanding the strategic plan to include partners, customers, and suppliers throughout the supply chain could introduce significant change management and risk management implications. The key is to focus on the present with a clear set of rules and guidelines to achieve the growth and success needed now and plan for the future to ensure that the firm is positioned to handle changes in rules and guidelines over time. By working out a timetable for producing and maintaining the c-commerce strategic plan, the focus will be on the long term. Stick to the timetable and avoid being distracted by operational issues in the short term. Understanding boundaries as a framing approach to problem solving and decision making is important to improving execution capabilities of organizations in which continual change is in play yet some degree of clarity for manageable action is sought.

Real-Time Collaboration Enterprise (RTCE)—
The Adaptive Organization

Real-time collaboration enterprises are virtual organizations with the ability to quickly align business partners and assets. They are able to deliver products or services through internal, direct, or outsourced models and exploit competitive advantage when new opportunities emerge. The two key attributes required to create real-time enterprises are: (1) business processes—moving from a functional organization to a process organization and (2) integrated systems—creating a technology platform that compiles and shares information and applications across the supply chain. Real-time enterprises are flexible and fluid and avoid restrictive, tightly coupled, static business relationships. Instead they use a more dynamic, loosely coupled, opportunistic approach that focuses on synchronization—bringing the right knowledge competency and information together in real time from within or outside the enterprise to most effectively and efficiently execute end-to-end business processing.

Real-time business is about interactions between employees and customers, among firms of all sizes across the supply chain, and between incompatible applications and information sources. C-commerce is designed to remove barriers to interaction, reduce risk, and improve success. The real-time collaboration enterprise is focused on three key capabilities: (1) coordinated activities of employees, partners, and applications; (2) information management to ensure data, transactions, and documents are available to employees, partners, and business processes; and (3) knowledge creation that leverages information and drives immediate change for employees, partners, and business processes. Firms of all levels of complexity will derive value as a real-time collaboration enterprise. The benefits are immediate, cost effective, and sustainable. Coordinated activities make employees, partners, and applications more effective and increase overall efficiency. The availability of more complete and accurate information helps employees and partners more quickly identify and analyze problems and opportunities. Knowledge sharing and creation allow employees, partners, and applications to be more responsive to events and conditions that represent opportunities to optimize value, performance, and learning.

Governance—Make and Execute Decisions

Collaboration requires a sustained commitment to four major principles: (1) mutual relationships and goals, (2) joint development of structures with shared responsibilities, (3) joint authority and joint accountability for successful outcomes, and (4) shared resources and rewards. The c-commerce governance model will need to manage: people and collaboration, business dynamics, and building and leveraging networks. There are several attributes that need to be clearly defined to successfully implement the ten c-commerce capabilities. The governance attributes to consider are the following:

- *Vision.* Define the short- and long-term strategy for c-commerce in the organization. This strategic plan will drive the timing and execution of the action plans and programs to successfully complete the business process and c-commerce initiative.
- *Leadership.* Leadership will focus on identifying and empowering stakeholders throughout the supply chain. In the early formative stages, leveraging consultants is often a useful approach to ensure all stakeholders are engaged in developing the business process and c-commerce initiative. The governance model will ensure that decisions are made so that stakeholders can effectively execute successful completion of assigned action plans and programs.

- *Culture.* The corporate culture will drive how the change management, diversity, and continuous improvement programs will need to be defined and executed. The success of the business process and c-commerce initiative will be the adoption of the culture to embrace the c-commerce capabilities.
- *Stakeholders.* This is the identification and establishing commitments from the key people required to successfully design, build, and implement the business process and c-commerce initiative in the firm.
- *Operating principles.* Operating principles are the guidelines for effective collaborative decision making and policy formulation to support and sustain the implementation of action plans and programs required by the business process and c-commerce initiative.
- *Commitment.* There must be commitment and dedication by stakeholders to work together toward the established goals, methods, and agreed-on decisions. C-commerce will become a new way of working together, and how challenges are overcome will be analyzed and improved on over and over again. Early adopters will become teachers and promoters for the business process and c-commerce initiative. They need to be clear on the time required and the level of commitment a program of this magnitude will require.
- *Service system.* The service system identifies the resources used for collaboration and includes communications, cross-organization resource deployment, and determining the response guidelines for collaborative problem solving. Good communication among the collaborative organizations is imperative to their success.
- *Financing.* The investment requirements to implement the business process and c-commerce initiative are needed (i.e., people, shared infrastructure, technology and operating processes, and communication). The initial information is pulled from the approved business plan and continues as a dynamic tool to manage the implementation of the program. Keep in mind that financial capital can only jump-start collaboration. Sustainability is achieved through human capital (knowledge, skills, attitudes) and social capital (social links that support human capital development and application).

- *Licensing and contracting.* How resource management and services are procured by the collaborative governance structure must be clearly defined.
- *Information systems.* Collaboration, content management, and knowledge management applications must be established throughout the firm to execute the business process and c-commerce initiative. Avoid duplicative systems and processes among collaborative stakeholders. Determine how information costs can be aggregated to optimize the efficiencies of the entire system. Ensure security and confidentiality are managed and maintained.
- *Evaluating outcomes.* Develop clearly defined milestones and objectives that will promote the understanding of collaborative processes and outcomes. Communicate the results of the program beyond immediate stakeholder groups.
- *Ongoing reflection and learning.* Ensure that there are effective collaborative processes for quality conversations, defining best practices, and creating "collaborative norming." Identify opportunities for ongoing reflection and learning in all governance, communication, and decision-making processes. Create appropriate feedback opportunities for leaders and stakeholders. Develop organizational learning and continuous improvement activities around the ten c-commerce capabilities.

CONCLUSION

Implementing these ten core c-commerce capabilities within the firm will ultimately change business models and will fundamentally alter the way work gets done both internally and externally. Sharing business processes and leveraging knowledge through collaborative solutions allows c-commerce to provide for increased innovation and cooperation with all ecosystem stakeholders (customers, suppliers, partners, employees, etc.). Collaborative organizations result in increased agility and trust-making that allows them to adapt to change more rapidly.

Embracing c-commerce rapidly delivers results by streamlining business processes; it introduces new cost efficiencies, increases customer satisfaction and loyalty, improves human capital productivity, and generates innovation for exponential revenue growth. Successful collaboration efforts by organizations include: minimizing duplication of efforts and services; creating a long-term orientation for safeguards; enhancing the development of a compelling vision that will evolve over time; mobilizing resources through diverse abilities and approaches; taking advantage of power in numbers; and generating improvements in trust and communication among customers, competitors, partners, and employees. To consider and successfully evaluate a c-commerce business transformation, evaluate how effectively the ten major c-commerce capabilities discussed in this chapter have been integrated within the firm.

To review, the c-commerce capabilities are:

1. Purpose—The driver
2. Identity—The persona kaleidoscope
3. Reputation—Character and image
4. Trust—The core value
5. Commerce—The knowledge flow
6. Transparency—Informed and committed stakeholders
7. Networks—The social nexus
8. Boundaries—The rules
9. Real-time collaboration enterprise (RTCE)—The adaptive organization
10. Governance—Make and execute decisions

In Part II of *Winning at Collaboration Commerce: The Next Competitive Advantage* we look at seven dimensions of the firm. The dimensions are governance, strategy, process, information technology infrastructure, people, culture and change, and measurement. The ten c-commerce capabilities are outlined in detail for each of the c-commerce dimensions. Discussions of how each c-commerce capability is traditionally applied within a firm and across the supply chain are reviewed with a look at how they are evolving and growing in the future. Chapter 4 takes a look at governance. Governance provides the cohesion to manage and coordinate the effectiveness of the seven c-commerce dimensions.

PART II

MAKING IT HAPPEN: THE C-COMMERCE DIMENSIONS

In Chapter 3, we looked at the capabilities associated with c-commerce and focused on introducing these concepts. These capabilities are both high-level ideas and new levers that can be used to steer organizations toward adopting c-commerce. In this chapter, we use them as guidelines to contrast traditional organizational design approaches with c-commerce organizational design approaches and also to identify and apply specific change levers.

Major changes, such as the adoption of the c-commerce perspective, will happen in large and complex organizations only through coordinated efforts across many dimensions. C-commerce, in particular, requires changes in the following management areas:

1. **Governance:** This dimension refers to how an organization ensures that key decisions related to c-commerce are shaped, including sponsorship, key operating principles, decision-making patterns, and program and project management processes. One of the most important roles of governance is to ensure communication programs are effectively planned to monitor the ongoing evolution of a c-commerce transformation.

2. **Strategy:** C-commerce requires new lenses to envision and shape strategic thinking. It needs to be less deterministic and more adaptive and symbiotic. Traditional frameworks (SWOT analysis, Porter's forces, etc.), although useful, are firm-centric and not inclusive of partners, collaborators, suppliers, and clients. C-commerce requires a shared-destiny perspective. New strategic planning approaches that leverage scenarios, dialogue, and complex pattern recognition will be needed for c-commerce success.

3. **Process:** A process perspective and approach is a fundamental enabler of c-commerce. Without it, activities, people, and information flows are fractured. Firms need to identify core processes and strengthen these elements through c-commerce.

4. **Information Technology (IT) Infrastructure:** Not even small companies can play the c-commerce game without the right kind of IT infrastructure in place. IT is not a driver of c-commerce, but its inadequate development within a c-commerce perspective can be a major limitation.

5. **People:** If old ideas about how people should behave and how they should be treated prevail, then c-commerce will not flourish. C-commerce depends on treating people as true individuals. This means understanding that people can play many roles and have many personas and can bring very broad experiences to the firm. Creating an environment in which people are allowed to learn and collaborate in multiple ways will be vital to retaining top talent.

6. **Culture:** In a c-commerce context, organizational culture needs to be more fluid and embrace diversity both internally and externally. A range of issues needs to be addressed transparently to enable the move toward c-commerce—including trust, knowledge sharing, reciprocity, networks, and conflict resolution.

7. **Measurement:** C-commerce needs a balanced system of measurements. Balanced scorecards are definitely in line with c-commerce objectives. However, c-commerce demands even more attention to the health of the broader ecosystem that includes employees, clients, partners, suppliers, etc. Intensifying learning and growth metrics will be a critical success factor for c-commerce because much of the enabling DNA will be sourced in the cultural fabric and quality of people's innovation capabilities.

In order to move toward c-commerce, firms will probably need to make changes in each of these seven dimensions. In this chapter, we use dedicated subchapters to investigate each dimension and help the reader understand the many capabilities that support change toward c-commerce. The c-commerce capabilities introduced in Chapter 3 provide the framework for this chapter, and each section analyzes one of the seven dimensions in the context of these c-commerce capabilities.

It is clear that the degree of necessary changes in each dimension will certainly vary greatly from firm to firm. Some changes are also more complicated and expensive than others, and some may be much more difficult to implement or even so subtle that they can only be perceived after a long and continuous change management program. We realize that because of the nature of c-commerce, no easy recipe can be given without some context.

Management is an art. Great business leaders are those who make sense of the big picture, drive major changes, instill a vision, and help their organizations to prioritize and execute strategic initiatives. The c-commerce dimensions presented in the following sections should help business leaders take a holistic approach to c-commerce and pull as many levers as are necessary, possible, and available within their organizations.

Each of the sections follows a similar structure, which includes the following:

- A brief introduction and context-setting.
- A table that summarizes the key changes in each c-commerce capability.
- A more detailed explanation of the changes in each capability.
- One or more small case studies.
- A conclusion.

We believe that governance is probably the most important dimension and one that must permeate and integrate with all others. C-commerce initiatives rely heavily on effective governance. Good governance aligns strategy and operational practices that promote and sustain the aspirations, goals, culture, and business models of c-commerce. Thus, the next chapter, The Governance Dimension, follows a similar structure to all other chapters of Part II, but instead of focusing on changes in c-commerce capabilities, it summarizes major changes in governance within the other six dimensions.

4

THE
GOVERNANCE
DIMENSION

Governance matters. Recent studies have shown that strong corporate governance (defined by strong shareholder rights) is clearly related to investors' return, the value of the firm, profits, growth, and operational performance (Gompers and Ishii 2003). Governance in a broad sense can be defined as a form of collective government of the interests of different stakeholders involved in multiple relationships. It defines power-sharing, authority, roles, responsibilities, rights, and decision-making processes. These are the formal aspects of governance. Equally important are the informal aspects of governance such as higher goals, expected behaviors, norms, recommendations, and standards.

Governance is also vitally important to c-commerce organizations. In fact, the success of c-commerce initiatives relies on effective governance. Good governance aligns strategy and operational practices to support the creation, development, and sustaining powers of c-commerce. It includes decision-making bodies and rules to help organizations overcome the inherent risks associated with collaboration and the ongoing management of uncertainty, complexity, and changing market conditions. How responsibilities are organized, who has accountability for results, and who is accountable for decisions are incorporated into governance. Good governance models help individual organizations in a network to make decisions that balance short-term and long-term objectives. They also help balance each individual organization's goals with the overall goals of the network.

Successful governance models help all stakeholders expand their reach, competencies, and resources; they help improve information and knowledge sharing without requiring stakeholders to relinquish protection of intellectual property rights. Customers, executive management, process owners, process providers, service providers, and customer support teams are all involved in the execution of work processes and c-commerce. The more critical the work process is to the firm, the higher the number of people involved in overall governance and everyday management. Less critical work processes will require less involvement for executives, leaving accountability of relationship management to the process owner, process providers, service providers, and customer support teams. Decisions should only scale-up if the available competency is insufficient. This means that decisions need to be made as near as possible to where expertise resides.

STRATEGY—FROM FIRM FIRST TO CUSTOMER FIRST

One of the fundamentals of c-commerce is the shift toward placing the demands of final customers first. To deliver what customers need, firms specialize in a few core domains and rely on the network for complementary processes, skills, products, and services. From a governance point of view, this shift helps to harness the energy of all stakeholders and to reduce conflicts.

PROCESS—FROM HIERARCHICAL TO DISTRIBUTED OWNERSHIP

Traditional governance is essentially top-down and hierarchical. In a c-commerce context, this scenario changes dramatically because information, knowledge, resources, and processes are shared more extensively. Also, cross-organizational and virtual teams are much more prevalent. Processes are therefore managed in a more distributed fashion and leadership is more closely linked to specific competencies, skills, and the ability to act rapidly.

INFORMATION TECHNOLOGY—FROM CLOSED AND PROPRIETARY TO OPEN AND STANDARDS

Determining what information and knowledge will be shared in a timely and open manner is a key aspect of c-commerce governance. Also critical is determining how information costs can be aggregated to optimize the efficiencies of the entire landscape of systems and ensure that performance, accessibility, security, scalability, and extensibility are reasonably maintained. The goals of governance also include avoiding duplicated systems and redundant processes among collaborative stakeholders. To achieve all these goals, it is critical that all stakeholders fund a common platform for exchanges and/or adhere to open protocols and standards.

PEOPLE—FROM RESOURCE MANAGEMENT TO PARTNERSHIP MANAGEMENT

Enterprise objectives are defined when short-term and long-term budgets are established. Today organizations focus on the skills needed to meet defined objectives through employee skill sets, consultants, and other physical and logical assets immediately available to them. The c-commerce organization will expand enterprise objectives to include value chain, customer relationship, and supply chain goals. To approve and accomplish value chain goals and objectives, processes that incorporate partners, customers, and suppliers will need to be established where physical and logical resources are pooled, allocated, and consumed to maximize return on investment. For this reason, partnership management and its practices will become important for the success of c-commerce.

CULTURE—FROM PRESCRIPTIVE TO SELF-REGULATING

In a traditional environment, relationships are dictated formally and rigidly. In a c-commerce context, the relationships between players are continuously redesigned to take changing market conditions and unexpected events into consideration. Flexibility is the norm, and new players enter the network through seamless, nondisruptive processes. New formats and relationships are constantly being reconfigured in real time. Planning and actions are conducted openly with the input of all players. These interactions are usually facilitated by excellent infrastructure that allows for the exchange of data, information, and the expertise of all involved.

MEASUREMENT—FROM FIRM SHAREHOLDERS TO VALUE-CHAIN SHAREHOLDERS

In a c-commerce context, it is not possible to maximize the results of only one dominant player. Robust networks take into consideration the needs and constraints of all firms. Service-level agreements, however, need to be agreed on by all actors involved in delivering the products and services to the final client. The final customer's satisfaction is the measure of success. Within the limits of a customer-first orientation, there is ample margin of maneuver to allow agile decision making. These decisions need to balance short-term and long-term objectives as well as individual and collective benefits and losses.

CRITICAL ISSUES FOR C-COMMERCE

Organizations that leap into c-commerce without fully understanding the collaborative philosophy, different leadership behaviors, relationship networks, and service-level partnering agreements are likely to find that they have inherent conflicts deeply embedded within their operating processes. It is important for firms to avoid the marketing trap of collaborative promises. Solid foundations must be established for relationships that are value and principles based. When developing a governance model for c-commerce, there are three critical areas that must be fully addressed early on:

1. Licensing and contracting and operating principles.
2. The role of leadership and ongoing reflection and learning.
3. Change management and communication channels.

Licensing and Contracting and Operating Principles

The ways in which services are procured in the collaborative governance structure need to be fully determined. Clarity on the process boundaries of intellectual property is necessary to ensure that the overall governance operating models are successful. In many fast-moving industries, firms will need to move ahead without all the formal legal apparatuses to which they were accustomed in the past. More and more, important alliances are established that are based on broad principles decided by senior leaders. This does not mean that legal and formal planning is not required. C-commerce is increasingly complex and full of pitfalls in terms of intellectual property ownership, confidentiality clauses, and noncompetition issues. All these factors need careful management. Nevertheless, without the strong will of leaders that understand the imperative of collaboration and develop a common and exciting vision, people can get completely caught up in endless disputes around legal details and end up losing sight of the big picture and the need to forge ahead.

In this context, organizations will need to pay attention not only to licensing and contracting issues, but also to operating principles. Examples of good collaborative operating principles supporting a governance model include the following:

- A system that is driven primarily by market needs with everyone striving to adapt to customer demands.
- Shared decision making that is participatory and inclusive of issues and constituencies (including smaller players).
- Solutions that are equitable and provide benefits for all stakeholders wherever and whenever possible.
- Accessible, transparent, flexible, and open processes.

- Empowerment of individuals through a defined governance system.
- Priority for supporting higher order needs over those of individuals or subgroups.
- Final decision-making power that resides as closely as possible with the person or people most affected by the outcome of the decision.
- Informed, effective, and responsible decision making.
- Responsiveness as a key value.
- Promotion of collective decision making.
- Highly professional approach to conflict management.
- System-wide checks and balances.
- Balance efficiency, effectiveness, and flexibility.

The Role of Leadership and Ongoing Reflection and Learning

Implementing collaborative business models fundamentally affects all critical business processes. For this reason, the involvement of an organization's top leaders is essential. C-commerce should not be seen as a project, but as a corporate strategy. Developing a next-generation collaborative organization involves designing a business model based on new operating principles founded on openness, transparency, collaboration, real-time exchanges, knowledge, and innovation.

C-commerce requires leadership that is accountable for the following:

- The strategic alignment and prioritization of the work process and the c-commerce initiative.
- Defining and refining the primary business driver.
- Delivering business value through collaborative forecasting, planning, budgeting, and execution.

Who is ultimately accountable for the success of c-commerce and relationships? The answer depends on the level of maturity a firm has achieved for implementing work processes. If a firm is just getting started, it will often make sense for the work processes and relationships to be owned by a corporate executive reporting to the chief executive officer. The corporate executive can make objective and strategic decisions about where c-commerce integrates best with core work processes to improve business performance. This requires a perspective and responsibilities that extend across business units and across functional boundaries.

Another important role for senior management is to make sure that partners are committed and dedicated to work together toward the established goals, methods, and decisions of the collaborative effort. Collaboration exchanges are only as good as the individuals participating in the collaborative decision-making processes. Developing a clear understanding of each partner's commitment and motivation is needed for a successful governance sustaining process.

The customer will always be the most important relationship to manage. The process owner will ultimately be responsible for coordinating among the customers of the process, support organizations, and service providers. As the focal point, the process owner is responsible for ensuring that the relationships work effectively and making any necessary changes for improvements. A mature organization will have process management and relationship management ingrained in the practices of process owners to ensure that they are self-sustaining.

A department for process management, knowledge management, or relationship management will function in an overseeing and auditing role to facilitate knowledge transfer, best practices, and standards among process owners. Sharing knowledge in mature c-commerce organizations is not focused exclusively on access to common information sources. Planned face-to-face meetings are extremely important for sharing context, developing common goals, and building trusting relationships. One proven idea for optimizing this broader understanding of knowledge sharing is to have a relationship management office. This office encapsulates best practices and standards. It is responsible for the following:

- Mapping a detailed understanding of the primary business driver.
- Knowledge transfer of best practices and standards.
- Providing a link between customers, executive management, process owners, process providers, service providers, and customer support teams involved in the execution of work processes and c-commerce.

■ Portfolio planning and management, program management, project execution and management, and enabling capabilities,

Top management needs to ensure that there are effective collaborative processes for quality conversations, defining best practices, and creating "collaborative-forming" opportunities. This encourages the ongoing reflection and learning in all governance, communication, and decision-making processes. Continuous improvement activities are designed into the overall collaborative ecosystem to ensure organizational learning. The expectation is to move participants from problem-driven to vision-driven solution outcomes by maximizing resources and building sustainable outcomes into the way they interact with the supply chain work processes and complete their assigned responsibilities. A good governance practice is, therefore, to have clear and formal feedback mechanisms that ensure the review of critical decisions and of their wider consequences.

Change Management and Communication Channels

A well-designed c-commerce initiative is essential, but it is not enough to achieve full adoption and realize business value. Firms need to provide targeted adoption support to overcome obstacles and promote change. Adoption support should be targeted in several ways. First, different kinds of support levers can and should be applied at varied phases and key junctures in the adoption process to promote awareness, build and sustain motivation, encourage successful use, and enable full integration into everyday work practices. Second, adoption support should be shaped and focused by an understanding of the values, needs, challenges, and motivations of people across a number of different roles. Finally, adoption support and rollout plans should focus on the right set of people within a firm's user network and communities to create and leverage key early adopters and agents of change.

Adoption support that is targeted and based on an understanding of the adoption process and the needs and values of specific individuals, partners, and networks, combined with well-designed c-commerce dimensions, promotes early, rapid,

UNIVERSITY OF HERTFORDSHIRE LRC

and sustained progress toward adoption goals. At the beginning of the c-commerce initiative, firms should clearly define adoption objectives and success metrics and establish a plan to meet them. Baseline measurement of these metrics provides both insight into key challenges and a foundation for measuring the impact and success of c-commerce in the future. Routine assessments during the design phase of integrating collaboration into business processes should be followed up with continuous sampling of multiple indicators throughout the deployment phase. They enable management to identify problems that inhibit adoption and at the same time highlight underlying causes. This provides a foundation for generating potential corrective actions.

The elements used for collaboration include communications, cross-organizational resource deployment, and determining the response guidelines for collaborative problem solving. Good communications among the collaborative organizations are imperative for success. A clearly defined communication process is required to deal with "turf"-related issues, so all collaborative stakeholders develop a sensitivity and openness about all the concerns about roles and responsibilities. Communication procedures will ensure early, frank discussions to clear the air over any issue that may arise in the course of the collaboration activities. Sustaining adequate learning and knowledge sharing requires purposeful, continual attention.

GOVERNANCE AND LEVERS OF C-COMMERCE

Governance in a c-commerce environment also adds a number of very different perspectives to the key levers of c-commerce that were discussed in this chapter: strategy, process, IT, people, culture, and measurement. The detailed implications in each one of these dimensions is summarized in Figure 4–1, with further discussion in this chapter's case studies and in following chapters.

Governance

	Traditional Approach	C-Commerce Approach
⊃ Strategy	Firm First	Customer First
⊃ Process	Hierarchical Ownership	Distributed Ownership
⊃ IT	Closed and Proprietary	Open and Standards
⊃ People	Resource Management	Partnership Management
⊃ Culture	Prescriptive	Self-Regulating
⊃ Measurement	Firm Shareholder	Value Chain Shareholders

Figure 4–1
Governance Shifts

Visa

The story of Visa is often overlooked, but it is one of the most interesting cases of collaboration among competing firms in a fiercely competitive environment such as the financial sector. Visa was shaped under the leadership of Dee Hock, who hailed from a small bank in Seattle in the late 1960s. Until then, different banks had different cards, different payment systems, different service arrangements, and different relationships with merchants. Hock and a few others made history by developing the concept of a nonstock corporation that is simultaneously owned by its customers, suppliers, and partners. Visa, founded in 1970, is owned today by 21,000 financial institutions from around the world and accounts for almost 10% of all global personal consumer expenditure. There are more than 20 million merchants in 150 countries accepting the card as payment and generating the formidable sum of more than $3 trillion in annual card sales.

This phenomenal case of collaboration predates the Internet, but Visa has always been a strong advocate of ubiquity, technology-enabled collaboration, and distributed governance. It demands collaboration while fostering competition. It has strong principles but very flexible operations allowing constant adjustment for changing technology and a shifting business environment. Its affiliates are free to leave at any time, and governance is truly based on cells and jurisdictions. The firm has multiple boards organized in a nonhierarchical network system that is full of checks and balances; this guarantees that no single part knows the entire system and yet allows for a seamless global operation. The consumer does not know any of that—it only sees a direct relationship with the card issuer. Visa is the ultimate c-commerce organization!

The Counterexample: GSTPA and Straight Through Processing

The Global Straight Through Processing Association (GSTPA) was an important collaborative effort that held promise for the global securities industry yet ended up in a bankruptcy court. GSTPA was designed to be a common utility for investment managers, brokers and dealers, and custodians to meet to settle their trades. The initiative aimed to reduce the costs associated with manual work, failures in the matching process, and risks associated with default and currency exchanges. In the current system, the settlement of trades includes a mix of different systems, standards, and providers and a great deal of manual work and risks associated with volatile currency exchanges. The trade life cycle takes about 3 days from the placing of the order to the point where the buyer has the securities in his or her account and the seller has the money in his or hers. The goal of GSTPA was to bring the trade life cycle to 1 day, or T + 1 as it became known in the industry, and it was financed by a number of heavyweights in the global financial industry.

GSTPA lasted only 5 years (from 1997 to 2002), and it consumed $100 million and a lot of energy and intellectual property from almost 100 financial institutions. At the end of 2002, shareholders called it a day after only 3 months of actual operation. What went wrong? A number of reasons have been discussed by industry pundits, among them: the poor economy after September 11, 2001, competition from a for-profit firm (Thomson Financial), the emergence of an alternative technological solution, the lack of a marketing and sales team at GSTPA, and low interest from buy-side financial institutions.

GSTPA had been doomed to fail from the start: There were major problems with its governance. It did not address the needs of all sides involved, especially buy-side firms. The decision-making process was long and unbalanced. Technology drove the business, and economic efficiency was not a major goal. People-related issues were, perhaps, the main problem. As Tom Perna, senior executive vice president with the Bank of New York, put it: "Once the project started, there were personality issues and a lot of individual self-interest on a number of parties getting into politics" (*Wall Street & Technology* 2002).

CONCLUSION

In any c-commerce effort, the relationships established define the anticipated business value of any customer-focused core work process initiative. The ongoing management and operation of these work processes requires long-term relationships and perspectives while allowing for individual firms to seamlessly enter and leave the network. Optimizing and managing the adoption of c-commerce requires linking assessment with a sound governance framework.

The governance framework should include a clear management structure, defined accountabilities, and a simple continuous improvement process for prioritizing problems and opportunities and for formulating targeted action plans. The challenge is to ensure that c-commerce within a firm is useful, compelling, and achieves full adoption by targeted audience members as part of the way they accomplish their work. Organizations can meet this challenge and optimize adoption and business value by systematically applying people-centered design, dynamic targeted adoption support initiatives, and a sound adoption assessment and management program.

5

THE STRATEGY
DIMENSION

Chief executives and leaders need to start preparing their organizations for the realities of c-commerce. Their collaborative conversations must be designed and built transparently into their business processes to ensure their future survival. Leading from the top is critical for driving an executive understanding of the value of supply collaboration business models.

Implementing collaborative business models fundamentally affects all business processes. It is not just a project but a corporate strategy to design a next-generation business model based on new operating principles in which openness, transparency, collaboration, real time, knowledge, and innovation are at the core of the collaborative organization.

There are major shifts that all organizations need to pay attention to when formulating a strategy based on collaboration (see Figure 5–2). This chapter will address each one of these shifts and macro-strategy drivers and then will discuss the choices that organizations need to make to differentiate themselves from competitors.

Governance

	Traditional Approach	C-Commerce Approach
⊃ **Strategy**	Firm First	Customer First
⊃ **Process**	Hierarchical Ownership	Distributed Ownership
⊃ **IT**	Closed and Proprietary	Open and Standards
⊃ **People**	Resource Management	Partnership Management
⊃ **Culture**	Prescriptive	Self-Regulating
⊃ **Measurement**	Firm Shareholder	Value Chain Shareholders

Figure 5–1
Strategy Dimensions

Strategy

	Traditional Approach	C-Commerce Approach
⊃ **Purpose**	Company versus Company	Network versus Network
⊃ **Identity**	Products and Services	Stakeholders
⊃ **Reputation**	Easy to Manage	Complex to Manage
⊃ **Trust**	Underestimated Value	Core Value
⊃ **Commerce**	Win-Lose	Win-Win
⊃ **Transparency**	Competitive Intelligence and Protection	Shared Intelligence and Risk Management
⊃ **Networks**	Source of Cost	Source of Growth
⊃ **Boundaries**	Local	Global
⊃ **Real-Time Collaboration**	Slow and Cyclical	Fast and Iterative
⊃ **Governance**	Easy to Manage	Complex to Manage

Figure 5–2
Strategy and Collaboration

PURPOSE—FROM FIRM VERSUS FIRM TO NETWORK VERSUS NETWORK

Never before has the world seemed so small and the marketplace so competitive. It is no longer possible to think of competition only in terms of firm versus firm. The issue now is which organizations have the best networks to ensure their success. Confrontation is turning into cooperation, and competition into collaboration. No longer can a single organization adjust to changes in the marketplace without robust coordination strategies with partners, suppliers, and customers.

Collaboration requires tuning in to the business environment and constantly monitoring it to rapidly identify the potential emerging technologies coming from the same industry, adjacent industries, universities, and research institutes. Organizations engaged in paths of increased collaboration need an even sharper understanding of their own competencies, skills, and expertise, as a way of both protecting these assets and finding complementary partners.

It cannot be stressed enough how important it is for a firm to understand its own place in these networks. Some excel at integrating technologies, others at developing innovative components by providing superior process or manufacturing capabilities. Usually only a few firms are able to drive the innovation process in complex supply chains by closely monitoring and delivering the needs of final clients. Firms participate in many different networks as they broaden their competencies into new markets. Most are often better off developing a strong focused position within a vibrant network or integrated supply chain.

Highly sophisticated and profit-driven organizational structures require formal and informal c-commerce models. The objective is to focus investments on the firm's strategic differentiators using business processes as the framework on which to build a relationship network and collaborate across the enterprise. For example, Nike and Dell are collaboration leaders in very different and highly competitive industries. Nike's net margin of 6.7% is 50% greater than that of its closest competitor. Dell has a 10% cost advantage over the competition.

Enabling c-commerce and relationship networks for major end-to-end processes is still an early adopter's market. If a firm has an early adopter's mind-set and a business need, then it can achieve significant competitive advantage with c-commerce. It is important, however, to understand the risks and align management expectations with the state of the market. It requires collaboration with the individuals, teams, functions, and perspectives associated with the targeted, customer-focused work processes.

IDENTITY—FROM PRODUCTS AND SERVICES TO EXPERIENCES

Not long ago, firms that were mostly product-driven started to understand that service was equally important for their business success. Thus, they invested more heavily in customer service departments to take care of customer satisfaction. They hoped this would allow them to continue their focus on product development and sales. Soon, more aggressive competitors started to realize that service was an integral part of the product offering and themselves developed more service-focused organizations.

Currently both business-to-customer (B2C) and business-to-business (B2B) environments are being completely shaken by the notion of customer experience. It is clearly more pronounced in the consumer market, where leading organizations across a broad range of sectors—including Starbucks, Apple, golf courses, wine producers, and high-end automakers—are now designing their strategies in such a way that buying and using their products and services are just part of the experience they want customers to have and tell others about. The same approach is now permeating leading professional services firms and firms involved in B2B industries.

An experience, however, cannot be achieved without orchestrating a full range of well-coordinated products and services that will be delivered in a seamless fashion. The customer does not need to understand who legally owns all the products and services he or she is experiencing. The network provides the experience.

REPUTATION—FROM EASY-TO-MANAGE TO COMPLEX-TO-MANAGE

There is a direct relationship between a firm's reputation and the sources of its value. Firms clearly care if their reputation is threatened in a way that reduces their ability to conduct business.

Reputation management is becoming an important and complex issue as firms' sources of value become increasingly intangible and based on networks. Intangibles are by nature more volatile, and networks are harder for any one participant to control.

Managing reputation is no longer just a matter of producing good products and having efficient communication strategies. It is a daily concern that should involve all members of the network—internal and external. Reputation is also not only about pleasing the end customers; it also includes pleasing customers' customers, partners, suppliers, employees, nongovernment organizations, government, and surrounding communities. Although reputation is dispersed across all these groups, it must be a focus for top management. Top management should have clear signals, indicators, surveys, and hands-on experiences with stakeholders to actively manage reputation. The risk otherwise is huge. The case of Nike is interesting in this respect. The firm suffered immensely and had arguably permanent losses in reputation and, consequently, reductions in sales when the public became aware of poor working conditions in the factories it contracted to make its products.

At each interaction along a network, an experience and a story are developed. Leading firms will be the ones that have more positive than negative experiences and stories over the short term and the long term. However, as we all know from personal experience, bad news travels very fast: Really bad experiences and stories spread like viruses. Thus, careful monitoring of reputation and the ability to react quickly in the event of a bad experience or story is one of the key issues for success and survival over the long run.

Damaged Reputation: Kryptonite Bike Lock Firm

A recent case involving Kryptonite, a leading U.S. bike lock firm, is a good example of how fast a firm's reputation can be damaged through the speed of Internet conversations. On September 12, 2004, an American cyclist, Chris Brennan, posted a video message on www.bikeforum.net explaining how to open a Kryptonite tubular lock with a Bic pen in a matter of seconds. This message was followed by hundreds of comments and cross-postings in online forums and blogs. While all this was happening, the firm remained silent. A few days later, on September 23, the *New York Times* published a story titled "The Pen is Mightier Than the Lock," which took the story into the mainstream media. Many other media outlets were picking up the story. Kryptonite could no longer stay quiet. The firm first stated that its new line of locks was not vulnerable to the Bic-related problem. A few days later the company was forced to announce a major recall, offering free product exchanges to all current owners of tubular cylinder locks. Time will tell the final impact of this story on the firm's long-term reputation and its overall market position.

TRUST—FROM UNDERESTIMATED VALUE TO CORE VALUE

Research indicates that successful interactive learning triggers further cooperation. Firms that succeed at networking may become not only more adept at learning about the technological dimensions of collaboration, but also more skilled in organizational dynamics that foster open and committed yet flexible relationships with different players (Rycroft 2003).

Sustaining adequate learning and knowledge sharing requires purposeful, continual attention. Deep collaboration requires a commitment to reciprocity and shared destiny.

Organizations that choose the path of collaboration with third parties need strong skills in terms of holding open communication and in handling conflict as overtly as possible. In many fast-moving industries, firms will need to move ahead without all the formal legal apparatuses to which they were accustomed in the past. More and more, important alliances are established based on broad principles decided by senior leaders. This does not mean that legal and formal planning is not required. Collaboration is increasingly complex and full of pitfalls in terms of intellectual property ownership, confidentiality conditions, and noncompetition issues. All these issues need careful management. Nevertheless, without the strong will of leaders who understand the imperative of collaboration and who develop a common and exciting vision, people can get entangled in disputes concerning legal details and end up losing sight of the big picture and the need to maintain momentum.

Trust and risk management are two sides of the same coin in the context of collaboration. Trust is an important currency in today's fast-moving markets. Projects are increasingly risky by nature, and collaborating with third parties may increase the risk. Thus, sorting out who and what to trust is a skill that people working in a c-commerce environment will need to master to make fairly rapid decisions about entering and leaving partnerships and new markets.

COMMERCE—FROM WIN-LOSE TO WIN-WIN

As B2B e-commerce continues to become the vehicle for advanced supply chain management practices, the supply chain will be further redefined and tightened by offerings such as trading exchanges, hosting services, and e-procurement. AMR Research has stated that B2B e-commerce will reach $7 trillion by 2005 and is projected to be more than $20 trillion by 2010.

The competitive necessity of collaboration is undisputed as manufacturers increasingly outsource more of their product design to their supplier network. (For example, more than 70% of BMW car products are made outside BMW.) As this trend continues relentlessly, firms must be able to bring together their extended enterprise and design chain partners from the very initial concept stages in order to optimize innovation, capitalize on tight market realities, eliminate design errors, and reduce associated risks that impact maximization of profits.

At one end of the collaborative value chain there is increasing customer involvement in product development to ensure that products being developed meet or exceed customer expectations. At the opposite end of the collaborative value chain, original equipment manufacturers work closely with their supplier network to ensure that the final product incorporates the optimal components and multiple dimensions of product knowledge from key suppliers. This enables firms to deliver compelling, market-dominating products within critical market windows of opportunity.

Whatever the collaboration strategy employed, firms must consider how the network and final clients will benefit. The practice of squeezing suppliers still dominates many business relationships. However, in the most extended value chains, this is changing rapidly because businesses recognize that to sustain competitive advantage over the long run, they need to take into consideration how everybody can be a winner. Nowadays suppliers, partners, and clients often split the benefits that they discover by working together to solve their interface issues—be they challenges or opportunities for cost, product extension, and delivery improvements. Firms that embrace c-commerce rarely try to win at the expense of others in the network.

TRANSPARENCY—FROM COMPETITIVE INTELLIGENCE AND PROTECTION TO SHARED INTELLIGENCE AND RISK MANAGEMENT

With data showing that by 2010 products representing more than 70 percent of today's sales will be defunct (Deloitte 2004), firms that do not understand this new paradigm will likely fade away. Innovation requires a commitment and a comprehensive effort to open and improve channels of communications so that ideas can flow from anywhere. In this context, competitive intelligence is just a small piece of the puzzle; it is more important to develop a shared intelligence with one's network.

To support innovation, risk management processes that assess the health of collaboration as a source of power need to be incorporated into the available business models. Risk assessment audits will increasingly be developed within the work process and collaboration solutions. Recent research by Dr. Nick Bontis and Dr. Cindy Gordon (2004) has established a clearly defined enterprise risk management system for measuring intangible asset risks. The need for this solution is driven by the fact that more than 70% of all Fortune 500 firms realize the enormous value of intangible assets. These firms recognize that the customer capital strength of an organization and its associated relationship capital is a significant capability.

NETWORKS—FROM SOURCE OF COST TO SOURCE OF REVENUES

Traditionally, firms look at external partners, suppliers, and affiliates as a source of costs. However, there is another, more powerful way to view a network, and that is to see all players in the network as ultimately focused on servicing the final clients—the only source of revenues. This is a subtle difference in perspective, especially in a long value chain. But it is an important difference in how one looks at networks. Networks should only include value-adding actors. If one actor in the network is not adding value to clients that can be translated into revenues, then its product or service will be discontinued or reconfigured.

Networks can be a tremendous source of information, knowledge, and insights. One of the key roles of networks and partners is to manage, filter, and disseminate information to the benefit of all involved. Members of healthy networks understand this clearly and have a commitment not only to delivering products and services, but also to keeping everyone tuned into important competitive information that will ultimately generate new revenue sources or prevent the loss of current revenue streams.

BOUNDARIES—FROM LOCAL TO GLOBAL

Global competition is a reality in all industries, including cement, steel, education, professional services, manufacturing, and high tech. Very few industries and services are still protected within a local environment. For producers of knowledge-based goods and services, the need to rapidly diffuse innovation and conquer new markets is accentuated because such goods and services often require large up-front investments and have reduced life cycles.

Thus, thinking globally is essential even for some small knowledge-based businesses. Local suppliers, partners, and customers, although convenient, are not necessarily rewarding, and the allure of global boundaries can be very enticing. However, going global clearly requires more sophisticated collaborative skills and a much deeper reliance on networks.

Visionary leaders who have moved the boundaries of their organizations to a more global perspective have helped their organizations to develop not only their commercial competencies, but also the international outlook of their key employees. Doing business in different markets requires an honest desire to understand others' cultures, habits, and trust-building protocols. Building deep relationships, in the form of partnerships, co-developments, and long-term distribution arrangements, requires even deeper investments in terms of time spent on the exchange of tacit knowledge and relationship building.

REAL-TIME COLLABORATION ENTERPRISE—FROM SLOW AND CYCLICAL TO FAST AND ITERATIVE

With the variable costs of communication trending toward zero, bandwidth rapidly increasing, and the rise of process-centric organizations, technology integration and information-based processes are going to become the rule rather than the exception. Underpinning these realities is the emphasis on speed and the need to respond instantaneously to customer requests.

To be successful, leaders of real-time collaboration enterprises must work closely with business executives and information technology professionals to ensure their infrastructure landscape includes robust real-time enterprise collaboration capabilities. Numerous examples exist of firms that effectively operate in real time. Often cited examples include the following:

- Dell, with close to $1 million in revenue per employee, dwarfing the industry average.
- Wal-Mart, whose revenues exceed the gross domestic product of most countries.
- Toyota, which is now the second-largest global automaker.
- Cisco, which dominates the networking market.

In each of these firms, its dominance is directly related to its supply chain performance. These firms leave competitor casualties in their wake as they move forward. They are also the firms that have secure foundations of B2B and supply chain management infrastructure to apply more advanced collaborative formats for doing business.

The exponential reduction in cycle time is core to the idea of the real-time collaborative enterprise and is an important attribute of c-commerce. There are a variety of solutions and technologies that support the real-time collaborative enterprise. The objective is to trigger early warnings of events, ensuring the ability to reduce the reaction time to those events, sometimes to less than zero.

GOVERNANCE—FROM FIRM FIRST TO CUSTOMER FIRST

Firms continue to struggle to differentiate their products and service offerings. Organizations are engaged in a fundamental shift to a movement centered on consumers. They understand that consumers have choices and that consumer loyalties change now more frequently than they have at any time in history. What is the stickiness that keeps them coming back for more? Collaboration is what enhances the consumer's experience of a firm's service. Developing acute problem solving and listening skills, taking ownership of the problem, delivering on commitments, keeping customers informed daily of problem-resolution status, and aiming to resolve problems in less than 24 hours are basic collaborative operating strategies in many fast-moving industries.

The Royal Bank of Canada and IBM have been working together to simplify Royal Bank's call center customer conversation lexicon. Employees are trained to use collaborative ownership words in servicing customers. For example, "I care" gives the customer comfort that there is accountability and ownership, as opposed to the "royal we" of "We care." Saying "I hear what you are saying" (and repeating back the specific concern) demonstrates empathy, which, in turn, engenders trust in the customer that he or she is being listened to. Customers quickly ascertain the collaborative commitment through the quality of conversations they have with their service representatives. Their satisfaction with the product and service experiences will influence customers as they engage in the competitive war that rages to attract and retain their business. The quality of customer relationships is a key performance indicator to identify where customer loyalty lies. A new marketing war is unfolding;

one powerful weapon in this war is "collaborative language" used to secure increased customer trust, commitment, and loyalty.

FINDING A UNIQUE STRATEGY

To make c-commerce successful, firms must be clear on objectives, coherent about the strategy for achieving them, adept at structuring and managing relationships, and vigilant about accomplishing goals. Few firms have mastered all of these challenges.

There are four key motivations for c-commerce:

- *Cost.* Individuals, teams, functions, and perspectives that are focused on working together are much better positioned to capture economies of scale, leverage expertise, and manage the execution of process at lower cost.
- *Focus.* Firms that focus their resources and management attention on their core competencies and business processes that deliver competitive differentiation will be leaders in the marketplace.
- *Flexibility.* C-commerce will enable a firm to scale activities up or down quickly and to respond to unanticipated changes or new opportunities in the marketplace.
- *Customer intimacy.* Developing trust-based relationships with customers and forging increasingly personalized solutions allow organizations to lock in value-seeking customers and to put in place an invisible wall that the competition will not be able to climb or to see beyond.

Controlling Cost

Cost control is far and away the most important c-commerce driver among the firms surveyed. When a firm is working to control cost, it is concentrating on reducing the time it takes to complete work processes and using the least expensive resources available to execute the individual tasks that comprise the process. Firms will be focused on spreading the infrastructure investment across as many business areas throughout the organization as possible, investing in efficiency-enhancing technology and process improvements, and recruiting or retaining people with the appropriate skills.

C-commerce provides cost control benefits. There are hidden costs to the economies of scale and the specialization c-commerce offers, and a firm intent on using c-commerce to control costs cannot overlook these hidden costs. One is the cost of coordinating individuals, teams, and functions throughout an organization. These coordination costs can include evaluating processes and negotiating agreements in the form of contracts and norms among the individuals, teams, and functions; monitoring and enforcement; knowledge management; coordination; cost and performance benchmarking; information management; and day-to-day oversight. If a firm is considering c-commerce, it should calculate what it would cost to integrate technology systems between individuals, teams, and functions sharing a work process in the likely event that current systems are different. The good news is that the low-cost availability of communications technologies and standard interfaces based on Internet and Web technologies are lowering these integration costs.

The success of cost reduction efforts using c-commerce depends on how well both tasks and performance measures can be specified in a business case. While cost reduction can be achieved by decreasing quality or reducing service, it can also be achieved through c-commerce designed to improve work processes, productivity, and performance. It is important to understand the operating and business models at work in an organization. In general, this means understanding where costs are generated and how they influence revenue and produce profits.

A key question to answer when deciding on whether to adopt c-commerce for cost reasons is: How do you ensure that c-commerce will reduce your overall costs?

Sharpening Focus

Focus means to concentrate on a few core capabilities or activities and to try to outperform the competition in these differentiating areas. C-commerce is an obvious way to help a firm focus, and customers benefit. By concentrating on and executing core or mission-critical work processes that differentiate an organization from its competitors, firms are able to improve the quality of these targeted work processes. They are able to specialize and invest in the resources and expertise necessary to deliver world-class service for the work processes they focus on.

Among the business thinkers who support this resource-based view of the firm is Peter Drucker, who suggests that a firm should focus only on those activities and processes that directly generate revenue. Every firm in the industry value chain should concentrate on what it does best and maximize the value added.

A key question to answer when thinking about using c-commerce to sharpen the strategic focus is: How do you identify and develop the right mission-critical or core processes for your business?

Enhancing Flexibility

Many firms implement c-commerce to enhance their ability to access new capabilities and technologies as early as possible. C-commerce enables them to change the mix of their products, services, and capabilities through market relationships with suppliers, customers, and partners rather than by changing or replacing internal assets and capabilities. It also enables the firm to ramp business volume up and down as market demand fluctuates because the supply chain represents variable capacity and variable cost.

Seeking corporate flexibility through c-commerce has its roots in the "dynamic capabilities" view of the firm. David Teece and Gary Pisano (1998) describe firms that can adapt, integrate, and reconfigure their internal and external skills, resources, and functional competencies to match the requirements of the changing business environment. They hold that systematic change (in which there is a high degree of interdependency across processes and activities) is better handled by internal processes and management. Knowledge is highlighted as a key factor. If corporate knowledge is highly structured and explicit, then markets are better at providing flexibility. If knowledge is highly unstructured and implicit, then internal management methods are more effective.

Developing Customer Intimacy

C-commerce allows organizations to become completely customer-centric by focusing only on processes that have a direct contact with their final customer. All other processes may be left to partners. Customers will not mind sharing their needs openly if they trust that their suppliers will use the information only for improving the level of service. Sharing, however, works best when it becomes a two-way road—suppliers also need to be transparent about their capabilities, resources, and delivery options. It is through this open, two-way information and knowledge flow that customer intimacy develops and that organizations differentiate themselves by truly personalizing services and helping customers achieve their goals.

The customer intimacy option needs to permeate business processes, values, and the attitudes of all employees and business partners. It is an option that works only if customers feel that every point of contact will be fully committed to its satisfaction—no compromises.

Communicating the Primary Driver

Once the c-commerce decision is clearly linked to strategic business performance metrics, an organization must chose which of the primary drivers—cost, focus, flexibility, or customer intimacy—it will focus on. Three key factors define the importance of this choice.

- The primary driver clarifies the value proposition that the firm needs to seek as the key c-commerce and relationship networks objective. Articulating the primary driver enables the firm to define the mission of c-commerce and establish the approach in the firm's business performance objective.
- Defining the primary driver helps manage expectations, including the likelihood that it is not possible to achieve

improvements in cost, focus, flexibility, and customer intimacy at the same time.

- Once named, the primary driver becomes the focal point to unambiguously state the objectives for strategic c-commerce and relationship networks development. Change is always traumatic and often resisted. When a goal is clearly defined, resistance can be tempered and trauma reduced across the organization. In addition, everyone can be working toward the same vision.

JetBlue

Although it is a tough time in the U.S. economy, and in particular in the airline industry, JetBlue's performance continues to demonstrate dramatic growth. The airline carrier was founded in 1999 and has been flying since 2000—differentiated by low fares, satellite TV, and comfortable leather seats. It is the only carrier that has put together 12 consecutive profitable quarters, and it enjoys the industry's best operating margins. JetBlue operates 220 flights to 23 destinations a day, compared with American's 4200 daily flights to 250 cities in 40 countries. Revenues were at $1 billion last year—small compared to American Airlines' $17 billion and United's $14 billion. However, the firm is at a pivotal growth trajectory and hired more than 1800 employees in 2004–2005. JetBlue's plans included the introduction of a new plane into the market every 3 weeks in 2004 and one every 10 days in 2005.

Handling this type of growth requires some innovative leadership and infrastructure practices. The company's plan is to sustain the growth and ensure the imaginative talent around JetBlue will continue to support its ambitious growth targets. The firm's outline for its transition from a small firm competing in a limited market to a larger firm competing in an extended or global market is similar to the Starbucks, Dell, and Amazon models. Its success will depend on the flexibility, speed, sense of intimacy, and collaborative problem-solving spirit it is able to create through its network of employees and customers.

JetBlue hired Chris Collins as vice president of system operations; he learned from his experiences at People Express that one can stretch too fast and too far. It is too easy to choke on increasing volume when the supporting business processes and systems cannot rapidly scale to handle the capacity. Collins has developed savvy customer-focused work processes for routing intelligence. For example, every week JetBlue reviews the past week to ensure that the maximum time it took for customers to get their bags after departing from the plane was 20 minutes. (The industry standard is 40 minutes.) The firm has also invested in state-of-the-art technology to support its operational recovery systems. If there are any weather disruptions, the technology allows planners to rapidly select various goals before rerouting plans. The real-time operational mantra is "No canceled flights or delays beyond three hours." Software rapidly calculates a solution and determines a cost impact and whether it conforms to FAA rules. This type of program is indispensable in an organization planning to grow from 57 planes to more than 100 by the end of 2005.

More intriguing is the chief executive officer's leadership style. He actively works beside his crew members to generate a collaborative commitment and spirit for a great service designed to foster loyal customers. He flies with 8 to 12 crew members a week to internalize the customer experience. The JetBlue workforce is not unionized, which places the company in an enviable position to attract and retain talent committed to its corporate culture. Preserving the employee satisfaction culture that drives customer loyalty is one of the leadership qualities of JetBlue, which helps sustain this incredible success story.

JetBlue is setting new competitive benchmarks for other airlines by reprogramming customer experiences, leveraging innovative customer service and real-time commerce systems, and creating passionate and relationship-centric collaborating employees. Its success energizes other CEO peer networks competing in low-margin markets by reinforcing the idea that by changing the rules of the game there is breakthrough innovation and growth. Collaboration is a core competency of JetBlue's current and continued success. The firm's collaborative ecosystem maintains relationships across employees, customers, suppliers, and distributors.

The JetBlue business model's core collaboration purpose is the customer service strategy brand experience differentiation. To achieve this outcome, the firm has role modeled collaborative approaches in employee communication while restructuring operating processes to drive more margin into the business model. It has developed an intensity and commitment to preserving corporate culture that starts with new employee orientation; each employee contributes both to the customer experience and to the entire collaborative value chain. JetBlue knows happy employees that collaborate will create positive experiences for their customers. Employees understand the loyalty value to their long-term career growth and success. In other words, there is a holistic understanding of purpose working at JetBlue, with a core foundation of collaboration to create a unique and valued customer experience.

Retaining the intimacy that JetBlue has developed will require some careful knowledge communication approaches to its evolving business model. The firm is striving to create relationship clusters of competence and community of practice approaches to ensure continued knowledge sharing and transparent flows in its organizational systems. Managers know the secret is how people internalize the power of collaboration by working together to solve business problems so that innovation can continue to evolve.

CONCLUSION

C-commerce cannot compensate for a faulty business strategy. Any collaborative business initiative and resulting venture needs to link to the business strategy. Collaboration gives competitive advantage to those with a genuine value proposition to offer the marketplace. This is reinforced by discipline and reliability. Collaboration isn't a remedy to achieve the objectives of an already flawed business model.

Many firms do not sufficiently identify the primary driver for work process improvement and c-commerce. Firms should understand the core business driver—cost, focus, flexibility, or customer intimacy—to assess which c-commerce capabilities are needed to be successful. They also need to understand in some detail how c-commerce will significantly contribute to reducing cost, improving quality, or continuously refining the process to reduce cost and improve quality.

If, however, c-commerce and relationship networks are going to be used to address an immediate, short-term tactical disadvantage or problem, then c-commerce may not deliver what is expected and can even disrupt internal processes. C-commerce must be used for long-term cost, focus, or flexibility improvements. Implementing work process and c-commerce is no substitute for the development and execution of a winning business strategy. The key task is to build unique capabilities to differentiate the firm from competitors. C-commerce and relationship networks are guaranteed to attain these objectives by improving focus, adding capabilities, and reducing costs.

6

THE PROCESS
DIMENSION

A fundamental shift takes place when a firm moves from a traditional business process management perspective to a c-commerce view of business processes. The implementation of enterprise resource planning systems provides the initial movement to a business process focus from the current products and services focus within the firm. The transformation into a collaborative process organization occurs with the introduction of collaboration and relationship networks to drive how employees, customers, suppliers, or other key business stakeholders will complete their assigned performance accountabilities. C-commerce introduces alignment of shared values and leadership behaviors through formal, informal, and interactive collaborative communication processes. The relationship networks created build trust between employees in the firm, suppliers, and customers as visibility grows through consistent, frequent and purposeful interactions. How the traditional business model transforms into the c-commerce business model is illustrated in Figure 6–2.

Governance

	Traditional Approach	C-Commerce Approach
➲ Strategy	Firm First	Customer First
➲ Process	Hierarchical Ownership	Distributed Ownership
➲ IT	Closed and Proprietary	Open and Standards
➲ People	Resource Management	Partnership Management
➲ Culture	Prescriptive	Self-Regulating
➲ Measurement	Firm Shareholder	Value Chain Shareholders

Figure 6–1
Process Dimensions

Process

	Traditional Approach	C-Commerce Approach
➲ Purpose	Products and Services	Relationship-Centric Processes
➲ Identity	Functional Organization	Collaborative Process Organization
➲ Reputation	Product Experience	Customer Relationships
➲ Trust	Image and Employee Loyalty	Brand, Emotion, and Reciprocity
➲ Commerce	Product Lifecycle Driven	Customer and Supply Chain Driven
➲ Transparency	Closed and Dispersed	Open and Adaptive
➲ Networks	Power Centric	Knowledge Centric
➲ Boundaries	Clear	Opaque
➲ Real-Time Collaboration	Sequential	Dynamic and Iterative
➲ Governance	Hierarchical Leadership	Distributed Leadership

Figure 6–2
Process and Collaboration

PURPOSE—FROM PRODUCTS AND SERVICES TO RELATIONSHIP-CENTRIC PROCESSES

Firms will move from a products and services perspective to understanding the mission critical business processes and relationships required to develop and grow to maximize business and shareholder value. Firms are always balancing corporate growth with managing cost. In times of escalating cost, performance pressures force firms to examine c-commerce as a means of reducing cost, improving quality, optimizing the use of business resources and management attention, and becoming more agile in responding to new opportunities and changes in the marketplace. C-commerce improves the operational effectiveness of a firm's business processes by providing integration of knowledge know-how, richer experience and context understanding, and ability to more easily leverage talent and skills to execute performance goals. Because business processes define how a firm meets its objectives to achieve higher levels of customer loyalty, collaboration incentives are required to innovate, improve, and maintain business process performance at world-class levels.

The implementation team plays a critical role in turning the business case and resulting work processes into a win-win solution for the rest of the firm. The work process and c-commerce initiative must be handled in an open and well-communicated process, where requirements and commitments are cooperatively negotiated. If this does not occur, then additional time and energy is required to complete change management activities needed to ensure adoption of the shared work processes. Look for the following specific issues and create risk mitigation plans to fix them as needed.

- *Costs.* Verify that the business case and supporting performance measurements commit to reasonable cost reduction targets that all business units or firms across the supply chain are certain they can achieve. Recognize that increased collaboration practices support innovation and revenue-generating opportunities and that maintaining competitive positions will require investments in collaborative infrastructures to support collaborative work processes and work tool needs.
- *Capabilities.* Verify that the business case and change management plan will support the maintenance and improvement of assets and people. Make certain there are commitments to make the required investments. Invest in clearly defined new process capability models to help visualize new end state ways of working and behaving.

Ensure process models integrate with new people competency models for maximum alignment and return on investment.

- *Gaps.* Verify that there is consistent understanding of the business case. The objective is to avoid confusion and misinterpretation of missing details. These missing details will force unintended changes or a myriad of exceptions into the work process and c-commerce initiative if they are ignored. Be innovative and leverage stories to communicate the gaps; facts only tell half of the story. Look for the best approaches to achieving shared meaning.

IDENTITY—FROM FUNCTIONAL ORGANIZATION TO COLLABORATIVE PROCESS ORGANIZATION

In a traditional firm, functional business units define how an individual within the firm views his or her job and responsibilities. Conventional wisdom would have the firm establishing c-commerce for critical business processes and for those processes that define the enterprise's capabilities. However, to get started on approaching c-commerce, the firm needs to identify processes that add the highest and most distinctive value. Look for processes that provide a competitive edge and cut across multiple stakeholder lines: This is where the organization will innovate or increase competitive advantage more readily. By identifying collaboratively intense business processes, the firm forms the "signature c-foundation" of the organization; the business model and c-commerce activities will be built around these processes. All other processes can be prioritized for downstream c-commerce evolution. Securing early wins is always important in any transformational change program. C-commerce is no different. Individuals in the c-commerce firm will need to be assigned roles to perform activities and tasks within business processes that span across multiple functional business units.

A remarkable variety of processes lend themselves easily to c-commerce functionality, and a remarkable amount of productivity gains, innovation, and competitive advantage involves white collar and knowledge work. In financial services, for example, where deliverables take on the form of information and there is an increased need for real-time expertise and knowledge-worker access, many functions are candidates for c-commerce solutions. These include the following:

- Back office processes, starting with reconciliation of all kinds.
- Policy service and claims processing in insurance.
- Loan servicing and letters of credit in wholesale banking.
- Call centers and customer service for credit and debit card issuers.
- Equities research.
- Wealth management.

Sometimes several motivations combine in a c-commerce effort. A mortgage company integrated collaboration into loan servicing in its underperforming credit business to improve the underlying processes, return the business unit to profitability, and position it for possible sale. Building on the success of this c-commerce effort, the company is now successfully collaborating on mission critical processes that include loan servicing and its core mortgage business. The c-commerce strategy should be part of the firm's distinctive business strategy, incorporating plans for performance, flexibility, and focus for the purpose of innovation that is central to existing core competencies.

REPUTATION—FROM PRODUCT EXPERIENCE TO CUSTOMER RELATIONSHIPS

In the past, firms would base their reputation almost entirely on their product. In the c-commerce firm of the future, the quality and depth of customer relationships and partnerships will become the cornerstone of the organization. When determining the candidate business processes on which to focus collaboration activities, consider the characteristics of the process and the nature of its deliverables. Is there a physical deliverable or a service that must be performed in person? Are there multiple stakeholders and touch points in the process continuum? Or is the deliverable essentially composed of information? Does it have limited need for human judgment or intervention? To what degree can the process be performed electronically and therefore from anywhere? Consider integrating c-commerce when high levels of cross-functional participation are needed, when there is understanding and some degree of predictability in how the process is performed, when good documentation and information exists, when clear interfaces with related processes are understood, and when good automation of the process flow can be identified. Most important, consider the business motivations and goals with regard to the process. In other words, do not select business process areas that are not strategic, not understood, and have limited involvement of people. Seek out areas that lend themselves to collaborative opportunities to optimize knowledge transfer or create branded experiences.

It is both strategically and operationally critical for the process owners and other team members to have operating principles and guidelines for managing and governing relationship practices. This is especially true of customer relationships. Establish a dedicated group to assume responsibility and accountability for the end user relationship and experience. This will allow the firm to maintain its understanding of demand and manage the day-to-day relationship with the customer. At the same time, there are people in the organization beyond this dedicated group who will need to have contact with the customer and users because they can better understand their questions, deliver products and service levels, and resolve problems more effectively. It is not about excluding contact, it is about who ultimately ensures accountability for the end user relationship and experience.

A single point of accountability can facilitate demand management and make service provisioning and allocations more effective. Troubleshooting and problem-solving issues are avoidable, only if users are clear about whom to contact with questions. Support teams have to understand what part of the process they are accountable for and how they need to work with other members of the process. Having a dedicated group helps to ensure process changes as well as keep the process focused on delivering to established performance measurements and service level agreements. An additional benefit of a dedicated group is that unneeded services and other distractions are not worked into processes and relationships over time.

Trust—From Image and Employee Loyalty to Brand, Emotion, and Reciprocity

The word *trust* has many meanings. Often trust resides in the public opinion of the firm's image and the loyalty of employees. C-commerce expands the boundaries of the firm's level of trust-making to include suppliers, partners, and customers throughout the supply chain. It is critical that these extended relationships are built through complementary or shared exchanges to continuously improve and instill trust and confidence. People can always come up with reasons not to collaborate. The chorus is predictable: People have an innate desire to protect tradition, something that has made them successful or comfortable in the past. They say the firm will continue to be better off adopting or maintaining best-in-class industry processes versus experimenting with emerging or innovative approaches to business. The best way to work through this resistance is by ensuring executive commitment to treat c-commerce strategically and support the necessary operational process changes required for successful execution.

There is a big difference between purchasing products and services and instituting long-term c-commerce around a business process. The purchase decision is mostly about the product or service and its price. C-commerce integrated into work processes involves changing how people interact with each other and within work processes. It has everything to do with defining and improving relationships and much less to do with the products and services purchased. Clearly there is an experience correlation in play and brand over time is affected as a result of what process and collaborative relationship experiences create.

Business executives must be careful not to delegate too much responsibility around the technology functionality and c-commerce capabilities decisions to specialists in the purchasing department. It is important that purchasing specialists understand the principles for assessing potential products and services. Procurement specialists bring processes and methods for collecting information, performing the provider evaluations, and negotiating with potential providers. For c-commerce to be successful, managers from all parts of the business that will be affected must get involved in making the critical decisions, leading negotiations, and establishing the ongoing relationships needed to make collaborative work processes effective. The success of c-commerce will depend to a large extent on how the individuals, teams, and functions work together throughout the relationship. Hence, c-commerce requires strong participation and partnering involvement from all.

COMMERCE—FROM PRODUCT LIFECYCLE DRIVEN TO CUSTOMER AND SUPPLY CHAIN DRIVEN

Remuneration and profit is driven by the product lifecycle. Moving forward, changes that occur in the marketplace will require awareness, agreement, and adjustments by firms, suppliers, and partners throughout the supply chain to meet the demand of customers. What provides competitive edge varies dramatically, and direct competitors have very different value propositions. Within the same industry, one firm's distinctive advantage may be supply chain management, while its leading competitor's is sales and marketing. For example, many firms outsource recruiting and employee training, but for others, whose focus is flexibility, knowledge and experience provide differentiation. It is these key processes that will become the primary target to integrate c-commerce.

In addition to looking at the c-commerce potential of individual business processes, the overall business model and the associated management challenges must be looked at. Does the talent and capacity to manage the c-commerce change for the targeted work processes exist? To minimize complexity and management overhead, leaders must deconstruct processes into stages and facilitate a variety of formal and informal c-commerce activities throughout the execution of the processes. Learning for management and team members is introduced in stages in which they become effective and efficient over time and as they accomplish individual milestones.

TRANSPARENCY—FROM CLOSED AND DISPERSED TO OPEN AND ADAPTIVE

In the past, firms have competed within their supply chain, creating a closed system with decision making and control spread throughout the supply chain. In this kind of system, which has low visibility and a lack of transparency, it is difficult to know what is happening across the supply chain. C-commerce creates an integrated and adaptive supply chain in which risk and reward are shared by firms, suppliers, and partners. Information has to be available for people throughout the supply chain to establish high visibility and transparency.

The c-commerce decision must focus on business outcomes. There is a misconception in firms that a successful outcome is virtually assured through vigorous execution of the evaluation and c-commerce capabilities selection process. However, the outcome will be successful only if the motivations are balanced between customer loyalty and value creation and cost reduction strategies. If the goal is to build c-commerce into the core business process, the evaluation process should encompass both hard and soft measurement approaches. Ensuring that risk management scenarios are also taken into account creates additional benefits that firms often forget. What is the implication of doing nothing? It is difficult to measure or evaluate a firm's ability to innovate or the degree that it will be responsive to impossible-to-predict changes in the marketplace or specific industry; however, there is sufficient evidence on what drives a firm's ability to innovate and this is squarely rooted on the quality of its networks (Keeley 2004).

Some c-commerce arrangements prove disappointing simply because the firm fails to anticipate and adjust to life with collaboration. Integrating c-commerce into a process is never a simple flip of a switch. The firm's internal operations must adjust in the following ways:

- The people, processes, and technology working together to provide c-commerce process capabilities must adjust to upstream and downstream interfaces and include operational connections and communications.
- The firm's relationship management capabilities typically need to be expanded and perhaps enhanced. Relationship management is critical to success.
- Process management and improvement and performance measurement must shift to include c-commerce for accomplishing both continuous improvement and supporting enhanced innovation capabilities.

Networks—From Power Centric to Knowledge Centric

Firms currently rely on closed systems. This format requires that control or power be centralized on information availability for decision making. In the future, systems will be integrated, creating open environments. Once information is distributed and available, it becomes knowledge that is distributed and leveraged for decision making throughout and across the supply chain. To avoid risk, work processes should be designed and structured to support working relationships throughout the organization and in the marketplace so they are protected and managed. If an innovation objective is defined as part of the evaluation and ongoing c-commerce program, use relationship management to make the appropriate adjustments for changes in the industry and marketplace moving forward. The other option is to establish an innovation index as part of the evaluation and decide not to move forward with c-commerce if the inability to innovate is determined to be a significant risk.

Relationship networks are everywhere. They exist within firms, across business units and across organization boundaries. Even through they are informally constituted and reside within a specific area of practice, these self-organizing systems share the capacity to create and use organizational knowledge through informal learning and mutual engagement. The formal and informal relationship networks that exist throughout the firm and value chains are critical to understanding the complex knowledge challenges faced in transforming from a power-centric organization to a knowledge-centric organization. Motivate the firm to recognize the critical knowledge generated by relationship networks and clusters of people. These groups contribute in many ways to the health of the organization, including the following:

- Establishing shared work processes.
- Creating a sense of belonging and fostering relationship growth.
- Deploying the business process and c-commerce strategy through transformation.

BOUNDARIES—FROM CLEAR TO OPAQUE

In today's firms, individual accountabilities and responsibilities can be clearly identified. In the future, as systems become open and are increasingly integrated, it will be much less clearly defined where one firm begins and another ends throughout the supply chain. Current standard operating procedure is to clean up existing processes before attempting to improve or integrate them. Why? Because if the improvement does not address the root cause of what is broken in the business process, the result will be no benefits or a loss of benefits. Delaying the integration of c-commerce because of a poorly performing process may only serve to keep the source of the problems unknown, which will make corrective action impossible.

A better way to approach this issue is to understand how and to what extent the processes are broken and then determine what role c-commerce dimensions might play in working together to fix them. Is the problem poor execution due to a lack of skills, training, or technology? Or is it a poor process design that requires streamlining? The options for moving forward include the following:

- Target selected points of the process for improvement, then integrate c-commerce into the selected process points and measure any improvements in performance and cost.
- If the process is broken at the edges and creating havoc for connected processes, then c-commerce can be used to fix those interfaces and measure any improvements in performance and cost.
- If the choice is to create a detailed plan for process improvement, then use c-commerce as part of the new process implementation that includes a focus on interface building and benchmark testing.

In any scenario, it is critical to talk openly about the condition of the process. In some cases, the process is poorly affected by too many variations of it. Firms that grow through acquisition encounter this frequently, and most have realized that the best way to integrate an acquisition and realize the benefits of scale, savings, or synergy is to standardize key processes and their information systems. They use c-commerce as a means of integration to pull together the process, systems, or both and bring them up to design and performance standards.

In most cases, it will not matter whether the existing process is considered working or broken once it has been selected for c-commerce integration. We recommend that a process audit be completed to provide the basis and documentation for performance measurement and process improvement initiatives. It also uncovers the shadow processes. These are the undocumented procedures and shortcuts that may accompany the daily execution of a process or compensate for its shortcomings. When implementing c-commerce into selected business processes, firms should factor in how to dismantle shadow processes.

REAL-TIME COLLABORATION ENTERPRISE—FROM SEQUENTIAL TO DYNAMIC AND ITERATIVE

Closed systems require the extraction, transformation, load, and move of information for the creation of data sources used to manage performance. This process requires a significant amount of resource management to schedule when and what information will be available for use by the firm. C-commerce and the continued improvements in technology over time will allow for open systems and enterprise architectures to support interactive and integrated business processes. These improvements will expand exponentially when information is available for decision makers throughout the supply chain.

Often firms are looking for a silver bullet—a single application that will implement and accomplish their work process and c-commerce objectives. There is no such thing. Technologies must be used in combination to create the desired end result of a transparent delivery of work process, performance measurement, and collaboration. Rather than looking for an application or vendor, consider the c-commerce capabilities required to meet user and business requirements. Match the c-commerce capabilities that users and business areas will need with the technology functionality currently available in the information technology landscape. (This is covered in more detail Chapter 7) Consider creating storyboards to visualize how users will interact in work processes that support integrated performance measurement and collaboration.

GOVERNANCE—FROM HIERARCHICAL LEADERSHIP TO DISTRIBUTED LEADERSHIP

In a traditional firm, a strong hierarchical structure exists for the purpose of executing business processes and making decisions. The c-commerce organization of the future will distribute decision making throughout the supply chain and across multiple firms. This will be possible through the pervasive filtering, categorization, and availability of information and a defined governance model allowing virtual, cross-functional teams to make well-informed decisions.

Often a firm must adjust in subtle or systemic ways for mission critical processes that integrate c-commerce. These adjustments include the following:

- The planning and management of products and services, supply chain and production, or customer service may need to change to better interface with processes that have integrated c-commerce.
- If the firm will rely on c-commerce, then a training ground for managers and versatile teams that includes relationship management skill sets will need to be available.
- The overall financial management and governance of the enterprise will need to change as the business model leverages and relies upon relationship management.

Lack of specific transition and change management plans can compromise a c-commerce initiative. The plan should account for all the possible adjustments listed previously, including changes to employee behaviors and incentives. It should allow a reasonable amount of time to make these adjustments, and it should be structured as a series of steps and milestones. The most common mistake is assuming that the transition will happen quickly. Some firms merely try to cope with c-commerce. Smart ones use it as a lever to improve business focus, performance, and value.

Leaders and managers that are driving c-commerce into business processes will need to establish a collection of best practices to guide employees, suppliers, customers, and partners through the transition. To encourage and reward the desired behavior changes, managers should establish a collection of best practices. Every firm's best practices will be unique and designed specifically around the behaviors the firm is targeting for change.

THE VALUE PROPOSITION

The collections of core processes that define a firm and differentiate the organization in the marketplace are where c-commerce activities need to be focused. Becoming proficient at work processes can be extremely challenging, but effective organizational preparation and relationship management can mitigate the risks. There are several reasons to focus c-commerce efforts around work process. These include the following:

- Process provides the appropriate foundation for individuals, teams, functions, and perspectives to come together and work collectively to meet customer needs.
- Firms are becoming more sophisticated in their ability to manage process. This is a natural evolution and institutionalization of process management and business process reengineering over the last decade. Businesses and firms are being looked at as collections of reconfigurable and dynamic processes. The reconfiguration of work processes is done through effective collaboration and relationship networks.
- Process management has entered the mainstream, offering compelling cost and performance options for firms looking to restructure their asset and cost positions.
- Information technology landscapes that include knowledge management, content management, business intelligence, collaboration, enterprise portal solutions, and services eliminate the problem of physical distance. Firms with such landscapes enable work processes to operate and appear in intuitive formats for individuals, teams, functions, and other roles and perspectives to work more and more interactively and effectively.

Despite the strong conceptual case being made for c-commerce, many firms are struggling to reap the benefits of process and relationship management. Many firms have not identified their core work processes or accurately assessed the performance implications of their business models. Process-centric firms have learned to institute reward systems and governance mechanisms to ensure realization of anticipated benefits.

ASSESSING C-COMMERCE CAPABILITIES

The firm's business processes are the structure around which to design c-commerce. Once core work processes have been identified, determine whether the primary driver is revenue, cost, focus, or flexibility. This primary driver will provide clear directives on how and what employees, suppliers, customers, and partners will collaborate on. For example, if the primary driver is cost, then a strong focus on continuous improvement and operational efficiencies will be designed into the c-commerce capabilities built into completing activities and tasks. The criteria for evaluating c-commerce capabilities should be dictated by the strategic driver for targeted core work processes. These drivers include the following:

- *Revenue.* If revenue and profitable growth is the primary driver, focus on areas such as sales and channel growth, customer loyalty, customer retention rates, portfolio product and service growth, and channel mix.
- *Cost.* If cost is the primary driver, the c-commerce capabilities that provide time to market, economies of scale, operational efficiencies, standardized processes, and knowledge are key evaluation criteria.
- *Focus.* If focus is the primary driver, then quality and reliability of information assets, processes, people, and knowledge will be the most important criteria.
- *Flexibility.* If flexibility is the primary driver, the ability to change, innovate, and increase knowledge around work processes in ways that align with potential changes in the business and marketplace will become the evaluation criteria.

Identifying the appropriate evaluation criteria is fundamental to establishing c-commerce and relationship networks. A firm might be very efficient at executing its own processes but unable to respond well to any changes; the remedy here requires a better fit into the overall business operations of the supply chain, particularly when unanticipated shifts in objectives occur. Examine the firm's track record to determine its ability to adapt new work processes or products and services to the changing needs of the marketplace and customers. Following is a list of how key work process attributes fit into the knowledge innovation of a firm (see Figure 6–3).

- *Structural capital.* Structural capital consists of intellectual patents and property, methodologies, and software in the firm. Structural capital is the sum of the strategy, structure, systems, and work processes that enable an organization to produce and deliver products and services to customers. It is the firm's ability to respond to environmental changes and consists of the following:
  - *Digital capital.* The technology and software assets of a firm. The focus is on architecture standards, application

Knowledge Innovation

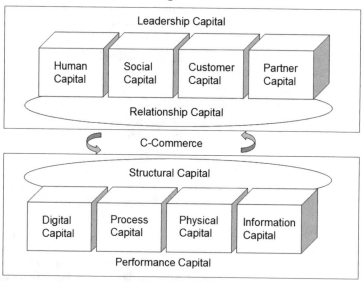

Figure 6–3
Key Work Process Attributes and Knowledge Innovation

integration, robustness of technology infrastructure, and disaster recovery for the purpose of managing codified assets.

- *Process capital.* Includes all work activities, including monitoring and reporting procedures that are required to perform the targeted process.
- *Physical capital.* The facilities, equipment, intellectual property, IT infrastructure, and systems necessary to perform the core work processes.
- *Information capital.* The specific functional knowledge and subject expertise needed to perform the process.

- *Relationship capital.* Relationship capital consists of leadership and vision focused on how human behaviors align to the purpose and strategic direction of the organization. It is the firm's ability to enable the creation of knowledge and innovation and consists of the following:
  - *Human capital.* All the line and support staff capabilities required to perform the process.
  - *Social capital.* The knowledge of the firm's strategy, business, operations, key people, and culture that define how processes are performed.
  - *Customer capital.* An understanding of industry best practices, common problems, and solutions to meet customer expectations and deliverables through the successful execution of the targeted process.
  - *Partner capital.* All the leaders, managers, and process owners and their compiled knowledge and performance records used to fully understand the targeted process and how to achieve results.

The key work process attributes and how they map into the primary business drivers of revenue, cost, focus, and flexibility are shown in Figure 6–4. Each should be assessed based on the firm's principal driver for business process improvement.

C-COMMERCE APPLIED TO WORK TYPES

Firms implementing work process initiatives and c-commerce are changing the roles and responsibilities of individuals, teams,

	Relationship Capital	Structural Capital
Revenue	• Relationship network orientation • Virtual team development practices and policies • Social network understanding • Partnership understanding and development • Relationship management orientation	• Customer intimacy orientation • Customer relationship management orientation • Information technology integration • Customer loyalty and retention • Quality of partnerships • Service level agreement orientation
Cost	• Efficiency oriented people • Management • Practices and policies • Cost model and leverage points understanding • Standardized process orientation • Operational excellence orientation	• Operational excellence orientation • Continuous improvement orientation • Information technology standardization • Economies of scale • Operational efficiencies
Focus	• Knowledge • People development practices and policies • Core competency understanding and leverage points • Best practice identification and transfer • Quality and expertise orientation	• Quality and expertise orientation • Ability to execute • Performance track record • Quality of asset management practices • Services offered • Quality of knowledge • Expertise delivered
Flexibility	• Continuous learning orientation • Strategic objectives and priorities understanding • Industry and strategic change orientation • Innovation • Change management orientation	• Content management orientation • Process management orientation • Asset management • Information technology architecture • Product and service variety • Innovation

Figure 6–4

Key Work Process Attributes and Primary Business Drivers

and functions. In most firms, work process implementations are delivered through employees of the organization following standard employee management by objective procedures. As c-commerce is incorporated into customer-focused core work process initiatives, these relationships need to evolve into partnerships. We also encourage designing partnership relationships into core work processes with suppliers and customers. Relationships need to be integrated into three types of work: procedural, heuristic, and executive.

- *Procedural.* Work that is highly structured and follows predetermined algorithms or rules. Employees have objectives to deliver specific levels, volumes, and quality of service. They will use their skills and perform their jobs on a collection of products and services to meet these requirements using necessary application and problem-solving capabilities as needed. Procedural work is most successful when the job and required skills are more complex, work processes are less complex and specific, and successful completion is well defined.

- *Heuristic.* Work that has little structure and requires a high degree of creative thinking. For employees to discover and learn to create complex deliverables they will form a variety of partnerships and collaborative relationship networks. The individual, team, supplier, customer, or partner will use a defined structure or collection of procedures to complete a variety of unstructured tasks to achieve a mutually beneficial set of goals. Heuristic work includes important knowledge for companies (e.g., human resource policies, procedure manuals, and complex sales contracts for new products).
- *Executive.* Work that is creative with the main output being decisions that determine a course of action. Executives establish organizational values, policy, strategy, objectives, and rules. A variety of formal and information relationship networks are used to continually communicate, share, and refine executive decisions and organization direction. Executive work is completed by employees of the organization with the responsibility to work on behalf of the firm.

For the work process and c-commerce initiative, the work types must be delivered by c-commerce capabilities that create an outstanding user experience. The services and benefits are a composite. A continuous understanding of changing customer needs enables the creation of more effective collaboration experiences with business counterparts throughout the enterprise. Improvements in relationship networks and collaboration experiences will translate into measurable business benefits. Design the experience that is intended.

Cisco Improves Supply Chain

Cisco uses a private, Internet-based supply chain network to create a global, collaborative network to link Cisco with its contract manufacturers, distributors, and suppliers through one central repository, streamlining all supply chain information and processes. Cisco encourages nearly all of its worldwide manufacturing sites and component suppliers to use this online supply chain network. The process of seamlessly integrating suppliers, contract manufacturers, and distributors into a single virtual enterprise allows the individual firms to achieve significant competitive advantage for the entire value chain. Cisco has had an Internet-based virtual manufacturing system for several years. In 2001, 70% of Cisco's orders were received and filled without involving the time or labor of a single Cisco employee. The results are annual savings of $700 million.

Cisco's objective is to provide greater supply chain flexibility and scalability. Using the Internet and shared processes to tie disparate systems across the supply chain, this global, collaborative solution eliminates information delays systemwide. With this solution in place, Cisco continues to accommodate its expanding product line.

The shared Internet-based solution provides end-to-end visibility and transparency for every firm involved. Cisco is using the better view of the supply chain to identify and plan for problems before they occur. The value chain creates secure and efficient processes for securing supply availability and on-time shipments to customers. Additional benefits include driving down costs and inventory levels while increasing supply chain productivity. As a worldwide data-sharing network (unlike in a transactional exchange), information is extracted from every firm's operational systems and provides an overview of interenterprise supply chain planning and execution processes. Using enabling technologies such as the Internet, relational databases, advanced planning tools, and open standards, different systems are connected to enable real-time information flow. The aggregation and analysis of this extracted data provides users with early advisories on supply chain issues, on-demand reports, and analysis of supply chain activities. Each firm is provided a comprehensive view of the supply chain. Each firm also provides early notification using alerts and escalation mechanisms so potential problems can be resolved before they disrupt the supply chain.

The Internet-based solution discovered an exception between a contract manufacturer and a component supplier: A part needed in January was scheduled to be shipped in May, or 4 months too late. The two firms were alerted and the issue was handled immediately, the product was shipped on time, and a potential line down situation was averted. The system has the ability to alert Cisco and its supply chain partners of delivery date differences, sales order changes, late purchase orders, aggregate demand, allocated part detail, supply and demand mismatches, and late trigger starts. It also shows details of the impacts of a given supply chain issue, provides linkage to affected customer orders, and suggests intelligent resolution options.

Every supply chain partner is receiving added value by realizing reductions in cost, time, and inventory at every level of the supply chain. The cost of doing business with Cisco is falling, and supply chain partners see improvements in key operational metrics. In addition, improved information sharing and process integration is allowing Cisco to maintain and improve relationships with its suppliers. Using Internet solutions to improve manufacturing processes, Cisco maintains its speed, culture of empowerment, and competitive advantage.

CONCLUSION

The effectiveness of the firm during times of changing market dynamics, new market entrants, and escalating cost and performance pressures are extremely important. If existing c-commerce programs are not in place to address these issues, the firm's effectiveness will deteriorate over time. In the future, to remain competitive in the industry or to continuously manage the firm's reputation, it will be necessary to distribute knowledge and leverage relationship networks to make decisions in the firm and across the supply chain. Consider implementing c-commerce capabilities as a means of improving profitability, locking in customers, reducing cost, improving relationship quality, optimizing the use of business resources and management attention, and increasing organizational agility in response to new opportunities and changes in the marketplace.

Do some analysis to determine which business processes are collaboration intense and provide a competitive edge in the way in which they are or could be implemented. Think about other business processes in which the firm would choose to invest in order to maintain or increase competitive advantage. For business processes that are already implemented, measure how well they are performing against a number of insight criteria (e.g., user navigation, learning and support environments, ability to dialogue with real-time experts at the process point of need). In summary, business process management approaches to c-commerce are a critical building block of intelligent and real-time enterprises. Harnessing the effectiveness of knowledge flows embedded deeply into process design and increasing people-to-people connections at the right process interface are all emerging practices to help firms transform into c-commerce–enabled businesses.

Chapter 7 introduces the information technologies infrastructure and links it to the ten c-commerce capabilities. The goal is to expand from a firm-centric view of business dynamics to a value chain focus. C-commerce provides opportunities to increase shareholder value for all firms across the supply chain with a focus on sharing IT architecture, open source, applications, systems, services, and business processes. C-commerce strategies must be combined with an information technology infrastructure to create network conductivity and enable real-time adaptability in a world where systems intelligence takes on higher levels of performance expectations as executives strive to increase agility in responding to market demands.

7

THE
INFORMATION
TECHNOLOGY
INFRASTRUCTURE
DIMENSION

The important point to remember regarding technologies and e-commerce is that the network, not the computer, is the engine. The network supports the processes that drive the continuing evolution into redefined business models. These networks find common interfaces to exchange information and make decisions, providing context in often surprising new ways. For example, the Internet grew from Web sites to extranets, exchanges, and e-business, and then into business process automation and integrated electronic marketplaces (e-marketplaces). More changes are on the way. Improvements in the supply chain, logistics, efficiency, and performance are constantly evolving. As network information technology (IT) becomes integrated, the number of available e-commerce-oriented business models and their scope continues to expand. Future business goals must

Governance

	Traditional Approach	C-Commerce Approach
⊃ Strategy	Firm First	Customer First
⊃ Process	Hierarchical Ownership	Distributed Ownership
⊃ IT	Closed and Proprietary	Open and Standards
⊃ People	Resource Management	Partnership Management
⊃ Culture	Prescriptive	Self-Regulating
⊃ Measurement	Firm Shareholder	Value Chain Shareholders

Figure 7–1
Information Technology Dimensions

support the exchange of commerce in a digital landscape. Two things are of vital importance: (1) Technology infrastructure must balance new levels in business process management, as outlined in Chapter 6, and (2) collaborating technology solutions, practices, and methods must be integrated into the business value chains.

Although automating certain functions and transactions, such as creating a sales order, can reduce cost, adoption is the key to success. It is critical that leaders and managers become avid supporters of usability practices; they must recognize that much of what has failed in technology deployments has been because of lack of focus on user-driven approaches. When deploying c-commerce approaches to meet the firm's needs, the focus must be on identifying a simplified, easily identified purpose of each user interaction experience, leveraging consistent navigation; this approach will result in dramatically improved productivity. Users appreciate when they don't have to think to complete common tasks. Using a collection of agreed to guidelines and common interface standards, user adoption and satisfaction will increase, and error rates, support calls, and training will decrease.

The organization has to provide a technology landscape that pulls together aspects and elements of several applications and solutions to meet business demands for faster time-to-market and lower cost for application development and integration. To remain competitive, the networks of people

IT Infrastructure

	Traditional Approach	C-Commerce Approach
⊃ **Purpose**	Firm Centric	Value Chain Centric
⊃ **Identity**	Functional	Integrated
⊃ **Reputation**	Reliable and Specific	Agile and Flexible
⊃ **Trust**	Narrow Picture	Holistic Picture
⊃ **Commerce**	Proprietary	Standards
⊃ **Transparency**	Application Centric	Personalized Delivery
⊃ **Networks**	Limited Access and Bandwidth	Multilayered Access and Broadband
⊃ **Boundaries**	Ivory Tower and Data Centric	Collaborative and Process Centric
⊃ **Real-Time Collaboration**	One-to-One or Many & Asynchronous	Plus Many-to-Many & Plus Synchronous
⊃ **Governance**	Closed and Proprietary	Open and Standards

Figure 7–2
Information Technology and Collaboration

and processes will need a digital landscape that we call the SMART Web. The application platform suite and the integrated service environment must sustain the supply chain and c-commerce process and networks, as well as provide a creative space to grow and evolve. The SMART Web takes advantage of the foundation of technologies available in the IT landscape to design and build service-oriented composite applications for the collection of business process initiatives (see Figure 7–2).

PURPOSE—FROM FIRM CENTRIC TO VALUE CHAIN CENTRIC

Firms will move from focusing on their own shareholder value by optimizing IT infrastructure and functions within their organization to maximizing business and shareholder value for all the firms across the supply chain. They will do this through shared IT architecture, open source, applications, systems, services, and business processes. Firms' infrastructures are evolving as a result of increased emphasis on collaboration across the value chain to increase network conductivity.

The majority of Fortune 500 companies have now deployed robust human resource information systems and financial accounting systems that allow for real-time tracking of employee and financial transaction data. As we look to 2006, continued investments in application integration will occur, and investments in collaborative tools to support cross-functional work teams will increase to improve their real-time productivity. Executives in larger numbers understand the complexities of unstructured documents and the critical need to develop enterprisewide content management strategies due to the knowledge embedded in Microsoft Word documents, PowerPoint presentations, and Excel spreadsheets. These unstructured data sources are increasingly the knowledge exchange vehicles driving decision making in organizations. Knowledge exchanges will continue to improve in productivity as more collaborative tools are deployed to support interactive conversations to solve business problems or develop new products and services.

IDENTITY—FROM FUNCTIONAL TO INTEGRATED

In a traditional firm, functional business units partner with IT resources to implement applications and services that allow employees to perform their jobs and responsibilities. Most applications in the organization were built by focusing on the data. This means that most business process logic is built directly into applications. The business objective moving forward is to focus on business process management. Process owners need to be able to model, create, monitor, and change the underlying processes as market needs change. The IT organization is accountable for maintaining the underlying infrastructure, technology, and application platforms ensuring that needed integration points are supported.

Individuals, suppliers, customers, and partners in the c-commerce firm are assigned roles to perform activities and tasks within business processes that span across an integrated IT landscape of applications and services. Integration capabilities are as important as business rule engines to manage process execution. Most organizations have implemented a variety of enterprise applications using several different vendors. Enterprise applications such as enterprise resource planning, supply chain management, and customer relationship management have incompatible data stores that create major obstacles for organizations as they try to coordinate business processes among various units. Organizations looking to connect disparate applications will have to rely on integration capabilities to bridge the gap.

Reputation—From Reliable and Specific to Agile and Flexible

In the past, firms would base the success of their IT solutions on how reliable they were combined with how well they met specific needs. These customized solutions take a significant amount of time to move from project approval into production. In the c-commerce firm of the future, success will be defined by how flexible IT solutions are in their ability to proactively meet shifts in the marketplace and quickly implement changes in work processes and customer demand. Firms looking to begin capitalizing on identified c-commerce opportunities should study the concept of the c-commerce IT platform. The concept encompasses all types of schemes for organizing information and promoting knowledge management. These solutions and services are used to categorize materials for the purpose of retrieval and to manage a collection. The c-commerce IT platform serves as a map between users and content, connecting people to people, content to content, and people to content. The objective is to identify an object of interest or information needed without prior knowledge of it existing. These processes of finding information are mostly interactive, with users browsing or direct searching for information, but the process can also be accomplished automatically as themes or collections of content on a Web page. This knowledge organization system supports creating collections of content that answer questions regarding the scope of information available.

One area where the c-commerce IT platform plays a critical role is relationship capital programs. Firms need to establish schemes to provide an overview of the human capital available, content of the collection, and retrieval. The common characteristics of successful relationship capital platforms include the following:

- Systems that define patterns and establish views on a collection of information and the objects included in it.
- The same object can be characterized in different ways depending on the expected use of the object and the collections in which it will be included.
- The c-commerce IT platform will support term lists, classification and categories, and relationship lists.

Trust—From Narrow Picture to Holistic Picture

In traditional firms, trust is built by establishing and growing relationships between business and IT team members. C-commerce expands trust by focusing on dynamic relationship networks. Successful completion of business objectives implies high adoption of online applications and the enterprise portal by users. To achieve this, the user experience is critical and must support targeted business needs. Adoption is much more than the number of times users visit the enterprise portal. Adoption of an enterprise portal or other online digital service implies that users can successfully and efficiently complete their tasks within the online environment. If users leave the online environment or channel to obtain the remainder of their service delivery through other more expensive and less-connected channels, the c-commerce program is not delivering on its business value and is not being adopted by the target audience. Adoption of the c-commerce platform requires that users turn to the online channel first and realize an ever-decreasing need for more expensive offline channels. The objective is to fully support business needs through the online channel as an integral component of critical business processes.

It is important to realize that users consume enterprise services for a specific intent or to react to some business requirement. Using or consuming enterprise services is an important user role that occurs within business processes. Users are not always clear or well informed about business processes, and they may not have the information that describes these processes or the applicable corporate policies. In addition, most processes require participants to make decisions, and they will need decision support. The best approach to ensure high adoption of process-centric services is to integrate business processes, information about processes, corporate policies, and other needed material into the enterprise portal. Here are the key characteristics of the enterprise process delivered through the online environment:

- *Alignment of services with user intent.* Users come to the online channel to complete a task or intent. The services are structured around how the user will need to logically step through the task. The online channel is organized by grouping the related processes and services, with support provided for users in selecting the right service.
- *A process oriented paradigm.* The online channel provides users with an integrated user experience in which the information presented guides them through the various steps of a business process that is personalized to their specific role. The process-focused digital environment pulls together and presents all the relevant assets to assist the user in that process. These assets include transactions, content, decision support, applications, and collaboration.
- *Online knowledge delivery and online learning.* As users interact with the business process, the enterprise portal also supports the user with knowledge delivery. This knowledge includes process-related information such as what the user's role in the process is, what the current step in the process achieves, and what action will result.

COMMERCE—FROM PROPRIETARY TO STANDARDS

There are a variety of challenges when it comes to supply chain management automation, end-to-end supply chain visibility, and supplier-retailer collaboration. The retail industry has been extensively educated concerning the benefits of collaboration, whether in the form of collaborative planning, forecasting and replenishment, or more generalized e-collaboration. Recent developments regarding the need to collaborate include the arrival of a long-awaited set of industry-endorsed standards. EAN International and the Uniform Code Council Inc. (UCC) have jointly introduced a set of actionable supply chain standards and an infrastructure and processes to support, maintain, and evolve these standards. The EAN/UCC system is an integrated suite of standards that addresses common data standards. Features include unique identifying numbers or keys; physical data carriers such as bar codes; registration and synchronization services such as UCCnet to ensure accurate, consistent information worldwide; and EDI/XML collaborative transaction management technologies to support order-to-pay processes.

Wal-Mart, for example, currently handles item synchronization based on the EAN/UCC Global Trade Identification Number and Global Location Number standard through UCCnet (a registration and synchronization service), with 40 suppliers. The experience of Wal-Mart and other retailers illustrates that there are standards that exist and will continue to evolve. Problems will arise over time from there being too many standards or from standards that are incomplete, problematic, or inconsistent.

Optimizing supply chains using XML and Web services standards is making it increasingly possible for businesses to share information seamlessly across diverse organizations. Companies such as Cisco, Federal Express, and Wal-Mart have invested heavily in Web-based business processes to support their e-commerce capabilities, and they encourage c-commerce practices in developing joint products and services.

Radio Frequency Identification (RFID) is the latest technology for communicating supply chain information. It is used frequently to identify the content of cases, cartons, and pallets, as well as actual items. With RFID, managers can follow items through the supply chain without direct line-of-sight contact. In the process, the technology eliminates the bar coding problem of line-of-sight, extends the use of the Internet, and addresses the serialization of products. The benefits include reduced out-of-stocks, reduced inventories, reduced mistakes, and reduced costs through increased automation. RFID shows great promise in early pilot implementations to streamline the retail supply chain. The technology still must overcome a number of hurdles before it can be widely adopted.

As retailers and suppliers implement EAN/UCC standards, they will be able to streamline their own internal supply chain operations. They will also be positioned to capture the benefits of increasingly sophisticated, automated collaborative activities in supply chain management and sales and promotion planning. Additional benefits will be realized through collaborative insight and product development in which retailers and suppliers work together to identify and create the products customers want.

TRANSPARENCY—FROM APPLICATION CENTRIC TO PERSONALIZED DELIVERY

In the past, employees completed activities and tasks using several different applications, information sources, and services. C-commerce allows activities and tasks to be completed using online environments with applications, information sources, and services blended together in the user experience. The c-commerce IT platform provides the glue to bring a combined collection of business strategies into a single system that links the individual initiatives together. If the focus is on collaboration, the primary business strategies to consider include the following:

- *Enterprise portal* is a window that presents information to users and a door that allows users to pass through to reach selected destinations and data sources. The enterprise portal defines the central location where navigation services are available for employees to find information, launch applications, interact with corporate data, identify collaborators, share knowledge, and make decisions. The enterprise portal has evolved over time to improve productivity and remove complexity. It is designed to create a bridge between the different and often disconnected applications, systems, and services to make work processes and finding information more intuitive for users. Enterprise portals are designed to empower people to access corporate information, find forms, open applications to perform their jobs, review a customer's project status, and perform many other activities from a single digital user interface.
- *Content management* requires the capturing and publishing of information in an organized way across the enterprise, with workflow and version control for managing

what is published and repositories for storing and retrieving the information. The ability to quickly find a person or any type of document, transaction, or report is the key objective of the c-commerce solution. Search, taxonomy, and the categorization of information are the most popular functions being deployed by organizations to meet this objective. The digital or Web-based user interface allows users to quickly filter and personalize how content is arranged, organized, and displayed.

- *Knowledge management* is the ability to locate and bring together people and relevant information to the individuals that need it so they can take effective action when doing their jobs. It is about providing depth and context to support effectiveness and efficiency and striking a sustainable balance between change and order. The knowledge management business strategy focuses on work processes, maintaining knowledge and facilitating communication, facilitating the use of current knowledge to focus on the future, supporting the organization's business objectives, promoting innovation rather than rework, and maintaining a knowledge-creating organization. Knowledge management practices will have a blend of both tacit (informal knowledge flows) and explicit (easily codified) forms of knowledge to support c-commerce solutions. Over the next decade, shared collaborative work spaces will become even more commonplace, with richer toolkits to automate workflow intelligently and connect all the required resources. Institutional memory will be created in all types of objects, and organizational knowledge will be more readily sourced at point of need.

- *Identity management* involves defining users with their own individual roles and privileges and allowing employees to navigate between Web applications without repeatedly typing in passwords. The identity profile information is used to filter and present relevant content to employees. Menus, navigation schemes, and the information presented in the online environment are all driven by the security rights and roles defined. A compilation of identity profiles, user roles, and privileges are created and accessed by Web applications and the enterprise portal to provide the single user-focused solution.

NETWORKS—FROM LIMITED ACCESS AND BANDWIDTH TO MULTILAYERED ACCESS AND BROADBAND

Firms currently rely on closed systems that have limited access and bandwidth. This format requires that control or power be centralized within the firm. In the future, systems will allow multilayer access and broadband. These changes will allow access to more information, through multiple electronic devices, presented in multiple formats, and with zero latency. Throughout this transformation, the scope and boundaries of c-commerce for the firm continue to shift and evolve. This has created challenges and opportunities. Organizations that have moved to focus on process need to capitalize on relationship opportunities and understand their specifics throughout the organization and e-marketplaces: the formats that exist for users to engage in collaboration; the roles that define the interactions and relationship support users need; and access to the interactions, applications, services, and information needed by each user role. The result is that a one-value-chain organization structure of relationship capital is created that can be used as a service to do the following:

- *Make better decisions.* The structure and collaboration servers available from the users' desktop should provide the appropriate detail and direct access to people and information in the organization for employees, suppliers, customers, and partners to improve and enhance decisions they make while doing their jobs and completing their assigned responsibilities.
- *Clarify semantics.* The c-commerce solution provides the framework to create a common view of the firm and value chain through the use of consistent terminology and navigation hierarchies.
- *Integrate information organization and search capabilities.* This characteristic allows collaboration to be integrated into the ways employees, suppliers, partners, customers, and partners complete tasks rather than around the applications they use. An additional feature is to provide search functionality to locate people, documents, and information available inside the organization or throughout the supply chain.

- *Offer direct access to knowledge and resources.* From their desktops, users can easily locate and incorporate collaborative interactions that focus on aspects of applications, data sources, and experiences of other people to complete their assigned responsibilities.
- *Offer direct links to reports, analysis, and queries.* Summarized or status information that needs to be tracked, published, and presented is incorporated into the desktop or digital environment. These reports provide several services that expand from information retrieval to educate employees, suppliers, customers, and partners to evaluating and measuring the success of the supply chain's performance objectives and defined metrics. Using collaboration features to react and interact within performance management can provide significant value to the firm and the entire supply chain.
- *Offer direct links to related or relative data points.* This benefit encapsulates the ability to traverse content through the digital environment that is filtered to be relevant to the specific responsibilities and interest of the communities and people that use and interact with it.
- *Provide personalized access to content.* Personalization provides the ability and functionality required for each user and community to organize, define the content available, and rearrange the digital environment to work effectively and efficiently.

BOUNDARIES—FROM IVORY TOWER AND DATA CENTRIC TO COLLABORATIVE AND PROCESS CENTRIC

In today's firms, the available unique IT solutions and services provide competitive advantage. These solutions are data centric and the knowledge about these solutions is contained primarily within the IT organization. The term *ivory tower* is used to describe this scenario. The IT infrastructure of the future provides integrated solutions and services that focus on core competencies, collaboration, and business processes. Noncritical business processes are outsourced when appropriate.

Negotiation among business units, suppliers, customers, and partners to combine and integrate proprietary applications, solutions, and services defines today's firm. In the future c-commerce will require agreements around business processes and IT standards to integrate shared solutions and services, stream data and content, and exchange open source. The enterprise resource planning solution is designed to support specific business processes and functions within the enterprise. Enterprise resource planning allows the organization to group individual users into specific roles with objectives that target screens, transactions, and other elements of a work process as the focus. It is important that the enterprise resource planning solution have a business process focus that includes the following:

- Targeted activities that are mapped into business processes.
- A collection of targeted activities that creates coherent, self-contained business processes.
- User roles and their interactions that perform the collection of targeted activities.

This business process focus of the enterprise resource planning solution provides the framework for c-commerce. For example, if the enterprise resource planning solution is designed to include various participants in the supply chain, then marketing, retailers, suppliers, designers, buyers, and merchandisers will all be able to track materials and products through the business process, focusing on the content, information, and other people that are relevant to their role in the business process.

The IT platform should be reviewed with two objectives in mind. The first objective is to determine what is available in the landscape with which to create a holistic supply chain and c-commerce solution, and the second objective is to identify where simplifying the IT portfolio is possible. It is important to complete a technical architecture analysis and organize the infrastructure planning activities. The information collected will allow clarification of the technologies that are unavailable and those that are common to the infrastructure environment. The supply chain and c-commerce technical architecture is a federation of enterprise resource planning, enterprise portal, performance management, knowledge management, content management, and online learning technologies running on top of the existing IT network.

The challenge of organizing knowledge is in the details; the resulting system will be unique for every firm. The vision is to tap into the value available from the wealth of corporate information assets and knowledge capital that already exist. The firm will have individual requirements for content, usage, users, and context. The final result is an enterprise content management system that dynamically assembles collections of information residing in hundreds of document formats, applications, and services. The solution relies strongly on a system that provides powerful and comprehensive information discovery capabilities that easily integrate with existing work processes and content.

Real-Time Collaboration Enterprise—From One-to-One, One-to-Many, and Asynchronous to One-to-One, One-to-Many, Many-to-Many, Asynchronous, and Synchronous

Although the use of e-mail and voice mail continues to drive how the firm gets work done, we have all begun to realize the shortcomings. There is the constant filtering of incoming messages, having to sift through long e-mail threads to understand the current situation, or having to forward and resend information because team members were excluded or they can no longer find information. Using the existing one-to-one and one-to-many asynchronous communication solutions to do synchronous and virtual teamwork has proven too time consuming and challenging to keep everyone informed. We still need these asynchronous solutions, but we have to incorporate some synchronous technologies to continue to improve performance of individuals and teams.

The investment in technology infrastructure to support collaborative processes and enable real-time connections is rapidly expanding. The investments in portals and enterprise content management strategies to connect diverse islands of information and knowledge sources are a major focus for all Fortune 500 companies, with estimates that more than 70% of these companies have active large-scale portal or enterprise content management strategy projects under way in their organizations.

- By 2007, the need for real-time business processes and measurement will drive the Global 1000 to redeploy next generation real-time processing infrastructure solutions that are collaborative in design (Gartner Group 2004).
- The portal software market reached more than $405 million in 2000, an increase of 128% compared with 1999. In 2004, this software market was expected to reach more than $2 billion (Delphi Research).
- In 2004, American companies were expected to have spent approximately $10 billion in information storage and distribution (IDC 2003).

GOVERNANCE—FROM CLOSED AND PROPRIETARY TO OPEN AND STANDARDS

In traditional firms, a strong execution and decision-making model exists between IT and individual business units, usually with a shared IT infrastructure for the firm. The c-commerce organization of the future will distribute execution and decision making throughout the supply chain and across multiple firms using a shared governance model. As users interact with a process and the related metrics, there may be various defined points in which specific kinds of collaboration will provide the ability to reach out and obtain, influence, or add to the collective knowledge of the enterprise.

For example, users could collaborate with service provider experts for decision support or clarification while working in a specific process. The online channel will integrate the collaboration tools right where and when the users need them. Another example would be sales managers reaching out to other sales managers for input as they refine the pricing strategy for a particular client as part of a proposal. Providing the necessary structure and process context makes c-commerce highly valued in achieving defined business objectives. The outcome of these focused collaborative exchanges will result in knowledge that will become part of the enterprise.

SMART WEB

SMART Web relies on a complete collection of Web-based technologies to streamline business processes. Features such as instant messaging allow employees to resolve issues and settle disputes in real time. We all need solutions that empower people to do more with less. Continued improvement within the supply chain and c-commerce networks relies on bringing together technology and best practices to dramatically increase supply chain productivity and efficiency. Faster implementations at lower cost mean that firms can focus on the fundamentals of running their business.

E-marketplaces are providing collaborative environments where companies can buy, sell, and work together on planning and forecasting strategies. These marketplaces are about promoting collaboration among trading partners. Virtual communities of designers, suppliers, and manufacturers join together to achieve several competitive advantages; these include the following:

- Improved inventory management and demand forecasting for raw and finished goods, enabling participants to take better advantage of more economical aggregated procurements.
- Improved supplier management and references that strengthen relationships and trust.
- Improved information flow and increased speed of delivery, allowing buyers and sellers to better respond to changes in market demand.

To support the behind-the-scenes technologies, e-marketplaces, and other c-commerce goals and objectives, the firm should design and build an IT-enabling framework, or SMART Web. There are several key attributes of the SMART Web. The first letters of these attributes spell the word *smart*.

- Seamless
- Measurable
- Access and integration
- Real-enough time
- Transparent

Seamless

The firm will want to focus on several Web-based collaboration capabilities: unified calendars to coordinate availability at individual and team levels; chat tools or online meeting room applications; discussion threads that focus on the outcome of a decision; document coauthoring and the ability to add annotations, vote, and set subscriptions; common deliverables tracking; delegated administration capabilities that enable any person to open a collaboration "room" without central administration or support; and robust searches for information mining and sharing. Collaboration functionality continues to be refined with improvements to usability, adding functionality that resembles e-mail, chat, and calendar interfaces. More important, these collaboration capabilities are extensible frameworks that integrate with document management, knowledge management, or analytical and transactional work processes.

Measurable

The user experience challenge is to ensure that c-commerce is useful, compelling, and achieves full adoption by the targeted audience as part of the way it accomplish work. Meet this challenge and optimize adoption and business value by systematically applying people-centered design, targeted adoption support, and a sound adoption assessment and management program. The pre-production stage identifies the teams and processes to be affected by collaboration and sets corresponding objectives associated with each process. (See Figure 7–3.) In pro-

Pre-Production
Objectives: Establish adoption plans; validate plans; identify process, tools, and people to monitor.
Measures *(based on business goals and best practices)*   • Stated as: quantity, quality, time, satisfaction   • Percent adoption across channels   • By business function based on behavior models with thresholds defined   • Quality measures   • Satisfaction measures

Figure 7–3
The Pre-Production Stage and Collaboration Impacts

duction, adoption analysis drives and validates the appropriate user interface for collaboration, ensuring the user experience fits the adoption assessment objectives and priorities. (See Figure 7–4.) Post-production adoption assessment actions evaluate the progress of c-commerce using tools ranging from online usage tracking analysis, activity tracking at the call center, online user surveys, usability tests, and applying best-in-class metrics from external sources. (See Figure 7–5.) This information is synthesized and used to identify ways to improve c-commerce on a continuous basis. C-commerce adoption should not be left to chance. Owners and stakeholders need insight into what is working, what is not working, and why. Continuous measurement and analysis of adoption progress provides the essential guidance that will lead to the desired results.

Production
Objectives: Design and build collaboration templates; incorporate user interface conventions; revalidate plans.
Levers *(things used to affect adoption)*   • Call center representatives trained and scripted   • Offline communication to users to support messaging   • Performance metrics communicated and understood (can be with or without rewards)   • Online tutorials and just-in-time training for targeted user segments available   • Online awareness campaigns   • Governance   • Interface modifications

Figure 7–4
Production and Adoption Analysis

Post-Production
Objectives: Ongoing improvements.
Tools *(things used to measure adoption)*   • Surveys (online and offline)   • Empirical data (Web logs)   • Heuristics   • Structured and unstructured data from the call center   • User experience testing   • External data (best-in-class comparatives)   • Interviews   • Contextual observations

Figure 7–5
Post-Production—Evaluating the Progress of C-Commerce

Access and Integration

Managers and team leaders will naturally want some degree of autonomy. Collaboration champions will be able to add the most value and wield the most effective influence by providing key services. These include electronic team spaces or room life-cycle management, centralized indexing, and security classification review. Team leaders need assistance at setup time to choose a collaboration template, provide the right metadata, and establish permissions that meet the team's needs and respect the corporate security policy. In addition, they need assistance at closeout time, when decisions need to be made about what needs to be archived, what records need to be retained legally, what team artifacts should become part of the firm's overall knowledge base, and how to integrate them into the enterprise categorization scheme. By intervening at these key control points, collaboration champions benefit stakeholders when their help is most needed and can positively influence the integration of collaboration into teamwork practices and business processes.

Real-Enough Time

When the information available to users is accurate, appropriate, and current, c-commerce will effectively remove time as an influencing factor. Issues can be transferred among support teams in different countries and time zones to "follow the sun" as each support team learns what has been done and continues the research and resolution activities. The current activities, their status, and proposed action plans are transferred in full to the new team, and work continues. By sharing information across business areas before decisions are made, firms can reduce risk, increase the success of projects, and eliminate rework by identifying and resolving issues that would not have been found until much later in the process. Providing informal and formal collaboration opportunities around information as early as it exists in a format that users can understand creates significant business value and profitability. Removing time as a significant factor through c-commerce improves work process cycle time, reduces rework and cost, eliminates risk, and results in better business decisions.

Transparent

Transparency will require moving beyond generic collaboration. Most collaboration solutions come with a series of generic templates suited to the purposes of projects or standing teams in the general sense. Portal teams and functional stakeholders should work together to tailor out-of-the-box collaboration to disparate needs. Teams on research and development projects, sales account teams, procurement teams, or strategic planning groups will have different needs, different work practices, and different related toolsets. By working together, collaboration champions and stakeholders, in conjunction with users who participate in the design process, can identify and deliver specific templates that support targeted business outcomes and align better to the associated business processes. The investment to transform collaboration into more than just a collection of features, to make it an effective enabler of streamlining and standardizing processes, leads to improvements in performance, profitability, interaction, and knowledge.

DELIVERY MODELS

Supply chain communications are failing. Executives are looking for opportunities to collaborate and improve communications in their organizations for the purpose of alignment, change facilitation, and engagement of suppliers, customers, partners, and employees. The implementation of effective c-commerce has distinct communication requirements; the work process itself is always in transition as each delivery model attempts to be effective for individuals, teams, and functions. The c-commerce delivery models are only appropriate if they provide sufficient knowledge.

There are four major and evolving variables in c-commerce delivery models:

1. C-commerce capabilities are either interactive for team use or persistent for individual use. As existing and new technology functionalities are made available to users in the form of capabilities, they can be categorized as either inter-

active capabilities or persistent capabilities. For example, persistent communication needs include synchronous application sharing, electronic whiteboards, message boards, instant messaging, wikis, and peer-to-peer network sessions.

2. Team capabilities are interactive and shared among users in the network. Virtual team members that work together in a network will share the same collaboration capabilities to effectively accomplish their objectives. The network of users will establish a number of group standards, best practices, and normal behavior and find the appropriate technology functionalities to use. They will often select only one or two capabilities and use them in creative and innovative ways.

3. Individual capabilities are persistent and unique for users in the network. Individuals will work independently of each other in very unique ways, using a variety of collaboration capabilities to accomplish their specific activities and tasks. The individual worker will use a variety of technology functionalities that complement each other. For example, if searching for information is not effective, the worker can start a discussion or begin browsing through a specific collection of documents or reports to find additional information. Individuals will use a variety of capabilities to achieve effectiveness.

4. C-commerce capabilities that force a disparity between work and benefit will not be used. Individuals, teams, groups, and networks of users will use a c-commerce capability only if they receive or perceive benefits in using the technology. For example, automatic notification of documents being added to a repository can lead to information overload; thus, this function will not be used. Other capabilities that tend to be more of a disadvantage than an advantage include individuals being required to maintain keywords in document repositories, virtual meeting schedulers, and alerts or notifications in general.

Use of C-Commerce Capabilities in Research and Development

Scientists were among the first, after the military, to use the Internet. The strong need to collaborate led many scientists to use a "green screen" to send text data and files across continents. Thus, it is not a surprise that the Web browser was invented by an American scientist working in one of Europe's finest laboratories. This involvement of the scientific community with the Internet continues. For instance, a recent survey of European scientists shows that up to 57% are using newsgroups (networking systems for identifying and commenting on research publications and findings) in their work and 52% use file transfer protocol for sharing and electronic publication. Almost all of those surveyed are using the Web for locating papers, colleagues, and initiatives, and 56% of them say that they are also sharing and accessing information locally through their intranet.

Scientists at large corporations are also using very advanced Web-based collaboration tools. A recent book reported, for instance, how scientists and engineers at ADC Communications, Eli Lilly, and Siemens were using advanced portals for looking up information, asking colleagues questions, and collaborating with people across the organization. Other interesting examples of corporate R&D Web-based collaboration include the following:

- Mondi, a leader in the paper and packaging industry and a subsidiary of Anglo American, has a centralized team that manages the harvesting, sharing, evaluation, and development of innovation. Its Web-based system, called the Innovation Zone, provides a space where ideas can be shared and improved on by employees. The ideas generated are accessible in a knowledge base until they can be developed by the firm or spun off as independent initiatives.
- Bristol-Myers Squibb operates more than 400 "knowledge desktops" and communities of practice, which serve as solutions for cross-functional, diverse

teams that work together around the world, especially with external partners.

- The Boehringer Ingelheim Group, a German-based global pharmaceutical organization, relies on a two-person knowledge management department within R&D. This department has paid a lot of attention to the development of knowledge-sharing tools (digital work spaces) that enable project teams to work more effectively with external partners in product development.

Corporations are also using new collaboration technologies that were initially adopted by teenagers, such as instant messaging and blogs. In fast-moving product development scenarios these technologies have proved to be incredibly useful. The examples of IBM and Microsoft are quite illustrative.

- Five hundred IBM employees use blogs to collaborate on software development projects and business strategies in more than 30 countries.
- A Microsoft product marketing manager maintains a Web log that encompasses 850 blogs and 1300 links that generate regular feedback to his blog from customers on how to improve Microsoft products.

Open Source Product Development

Open source is a new phenomenon that is shaking up traditional notions of collaboration for R&D and product development. Open source means that the content, substance, or code of any application is open to anyone to view, improve, extend, customize, or share within the author's rules. Yochai Benkler, a law professor at Yale University, gives open source a precise technical definition of "nonproprietary peer-production of information-embedding goods." The phrase also implies an R&D process that is collaborative and most likely virtual. Open source software is having a serious impact on the $90 billion software market and boasts more and more widely recognizable brands, including Linux (34% of Web servers), Apache (67% of Web servers), OpenOffice, ITRON Kernel, Mozilla, and MySQL.

An article titled "An Open-Source Shot in the Arm?" in *The Economist* argued that open source research can also have an impact in other fields and disciplines, for instance biomedical research and generic drugs. Open source research can be used to exploit nonpatentable compounds and drugs whose patents have expired and to develop treatments for diseases that afflict small numbers of people, such as Parkinson's disease, or that are found mainly in poor countries, such as malaria. In these latter cases, there is not a large enough market of paying customers to encourage large commercial organizations to develop commercial solutions. Some open source biomedical researchers have stated that should they find and patent a new treatment, it will be licensed cheaply to pharmaceutical firms to ensure a supply of drugs at low cost.

The same article provides a concrete example similar to the open source research approach. It describes how Dr. Peter Lansbury of Harvard Medical School is examining the therapeutic effect of 1000 approved drugs, most of which have seen their patents expire. His laboratory, which has approximately 25 researchers and an annual budget of $2.5 million, focuses its work on neurodegenerative diseases, such as Parkinson's and Huntington's, to which the major commercial drug companies devote few resources because of the small potential market. Dr. Lansbury refers to his work as "not-for-profit drug discovery." He sees direct parallels with the open source approach in that his group places much of its data in the public domain and its goal is to involve other scientists around the world.

George Dafermos has examined the management of open source production. He has found virtual networked organizations where geographically dispersed knowledge workers virtually collaborated on projects with barely any central planning and coordination. These networked projects shared a number of elements:

- They rely heavily on Web tools as modes of communication, with automated communications archives, mailing lists, and wikis.
- A large user base specifies requirements and participates in design reviews, beta testing, and implementation of new systems.
- Source code and other artifacts are available to customers—for them to identify issues earlier in the project lifecycle and to create a greater sense of ownership.
- More than 50% of open source developers participate in two or more projects, and another 10% participate in ten or more.
- As much of the development process as possible is archived to protect a team's knowledge base in the event of participant dropout or sickness.

With the exception of pro bono, government-sponsored, or pure academic research, it is hard to imagine large, for-profit organizations engaging in open source product development. However, paying attention to this emerging model of knowledge creation is a must for all firms. It is a process that, in some cases, can involve thousands of people across the world and generally includes young professionals motivated to be recognized as experts or, more often, because they want to develop a feeling of belonging to a knowledge community.

CONCLUSION

When transitioning to c-commerce, managers should consider the firm's effectiveness in its ability to optimize IT infrastructure and share information across business units, among partners, and within the firm. These interactions need to be focused on improving shareholder value through a shared IT architecture, open source, applications, systems, services, and business processes. Future benefits and return on investment suggest a long-term strategy for integration capabilities that bring applications, systems, and business rule engines together to manage and execute process needs. The SMART Web (seamless, measurable, access and integration, real-enough time, and transparent) functionality should be evaluated when designing the long-term IT infrastructure strategy.

It is important to capitalize on c-commerce opportunities and improve communication for the purpose of alignment, change facilitation, and engagement of partners, suppliers, customers, and employees. This is critical; the future will demand that execution and decision making be distributed throughout the supply chain and across multiple firms using a shared governance model. Planning ahead will be necessary to establish the IT infrastructure program and associated budget requirements needed to provide the c-commerce capabilities.

Chapter 8 introduces people and creates additional value linkages to the ten c-commerce capabilities outlined in Chapter 3. People are becoming more focused on how the tasks they perform are related to the goals and objectives of the firm. In addition, work is completed more frequently by virtual teams composed of team members across the globe and throughout the value chain. This diverse mix of people presents significant relationship-building and knowledge-sharing challenges. Implementing c-commerce capabilities offers significant benefits.

8

THE PEOPLE
DIMENSION

Lisbeth B. Schorr (1997) believes that settings that are most conducive to effective collaboration stress high quality standards and include skilled, supportive managers who hold staff accountable for achieving shared purposes and shared outcomes. In addition, "viewing people as strategic assets" continues to be cited as an important consideration of executive decisions. The importance of intellectual assets might be discussed in articles and white papers, but the constant reduction in training budgets and downsizing of operations proves that employees are still being treated as just another cost factor. The continued productivity drumbeat has created higher levels of employee stress. In 2003 Americans spent $26 billion on relaxation products. Yet, growth is made possible by healthy and satisfied people working with us or for us. Laudi Bassi and Danie McMurrer of Knowledge Asset Management have proven that treating employees associated with core competencies of the firm as intellectual assets and investing in their development increases returns over the long term. They have created and invested in the companies that spent aggressively on employee development. These portfolios of companies have outperformed the S&P index by 4.6 index points and the S&P 500 by 17% to 35%.

We predict that, as firms continue to evolve into process- and customer-focused organizations, not identifying people as a strategic asset will be a major enterprise risk. Employee under-

Governance

	Traditional Approach	C-Commerce Approach
⊃ Strategy	Firm First	Customer First
⊃ Process	Hierarchical Ownership	Distributed Ownership
⊃ IT	Closed and Proprietary	Open and Standards
⊃ People	Resource Management	Partnership Management
⊃ Culture	Prescriptive	Self-Regulating
⊃ Measurement	Firm Shareholder	Value Chain Shareholders

Figure 8–1
People Dimensions

standing of the significance of the transparency age and building a c-commerce foundation is critical for future growth and business value creation. Developing collaborative capabilities at all levels in the organization's internal and external ecosystem networks is required. Growth comes from genuine conversations that are rich in trust and reciprocity; this will support the successful innovation of new products and services (see Figure 8–2).

PURPOSE—FROM TASKS TO GOALS

Firms will move from a highly structured task focus of the competencies and skills employees need to an understanding of how the available skills and competencies throughout the firm are used for competitive advantage to accomplish operational and strategic objectives. Virtual teams composed of team members across the globe and throughout the value chain have a significant number of relationship-building and knowledge-sharing challenges to address. Process teams involve cross-functional teams in which individual team members have multiple reporting relationships. If they are global teams, then team members will be accountable for a matrix of internal and external customer bases. Firms handle this matrix-reporting environment in different ways. One approach is for the process owner and process team leaders to establish a steering committee of man-

People

	Traditional Approach	C-Commerce Approach
⊃ **Purpose**	Tasks	Goals
⊃ **Identity**	Single Persona	Multiple Personas
⊃ **Reputation**	Individual	Network
⊃ **Trust**	Power	Knowledge
⊃ **Commerce**	Transactional and Operational	Growth and Learning
⊃ **Transparency**	Six Degrees of Separation	Two Degrees of Separation
⊃ **Networks**	Business Units and Functional Teams	Business Processes and Virtual Teams
⊃ **Boundaries**	Formal and Physical	Formal, Informal, and Virtual
⊃ **Real-Time Collaboration**	Single Dimensional	Multidimensional
⊃ **Governance**	Resource Management	Partnership Management

Figure 8–2
People and Collaboration

agers to represent the various functions and customer interests to be addressed. Formal status briefings and updates are shared with the steering committee. An alternative approach is for each virtual team member to report status and updates to his or her local manager. The choice of approach depends on types of managers, types of tasks, and the level of ability of members of the virtual team.

Once the structure for reporting status and updates has been identified, process team leaders have all virtual team members approve material that is shared with management. This ensures that all virtual team members share a consistent story and are part of the reporting process. The process owner and process team leads will frequently create Web sites or publish information libraries to share knowledge and status information with the enterprise. This is an important activity that makes it possible for the virtual team's knowledge to be reused by others in the organization. Team members will follow standard procedures to publish information from their workgroup envirozment, including discussions, draft versions of documentation, decision-making activities, and research material to public sites.

Identity—From Single Persona to Multiple Personas

In a traditional firm, the single persona defines how individuals within the firm view their deliverables and responsibilities. The awareness of other business units and teams throughout the organization becomes more confusing the larger the firm. If there is limited awareness of business units and teams, how many individuals within the firm know each other by name and share information? Individuals in the c-commerce firm will develop multiple personas through the intentional development and maintenance of personal and professional relationship networks.

The firm is responsible for establishing the key principles of relationships. In addition, c-commerce capabilities will need to be tailored for the work types to be supported and the types of relationships to be established. Key relationships and personas combined with the firm's collection of c-commerce capabilities are used to design relationship network experiences. The collection of knowledge innovation factors is used to compile personas within the supply chain. The knowledge innovation factors include leadership, human, social, customer, partner, relationship, performance, digital, process, physical, information, and structural. The interaction of the knowledge innovation factors is presented in Figure 8–3. An example of how to focus knowledge innovation factors and personas used to design the user experience for procedural work, heuristic work, and executive work is presented in Figure 8–4. Several of the knowledge innovation factors are presented in the following list.

- *Human factors.* These are the experiences, qualifications, and attitudes of individuals regarding the presentation of information and processes. Users that are engaged in the work process must be able to organize, manage, and use information effectively. Personalization or user preferences might be required to meet a broad set of expectations.
- *Information factors.* The characteristics of information include complexity, ambiguity, relevance, and validity. These characteristics apply to the holistic collection of data sources used by the individual, team, customer, supplier, or partner to accomplish their assigned objectives and work process activities.

Knowledge Innovation

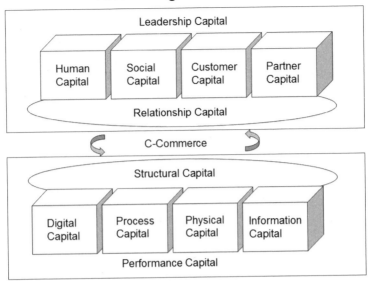

Figure 8–3
Interaction of the Knowledge Innovation Factors

	Procedural Work	Heuristic Work	Executive Work
Human Factors	• Process Portals	• Information Portals	• Dashboards
Information Factors	• Promotes the use of sensible rules for communicating • Information customization • Ease of use	• Strong relationship between internal and external data sources • Information customization with various levels of detail	• Compress, aggregate, categorize, and structure information • Visualization aids (graphs)
Process Factors	• Pre-defined decision models • Standardized procedures for interacting with information • Collaboration built into process	• Appropriate media for obtaining information • Refinement of search-results • Tools to enable understanding and use of information • Collaboration with information specialists	• Simple information retrieval and processing strategy • Regulate the flow of information • Measurement system for information and knowledge
Social Factors	• Increase in information processing capacity	• Coordination of information research	• Reduce divergence among the expectations of people
Relationship Factors	• Intelligent agents • Subscribe to information sources • Voting capabilities	• Group support system • Filtering to improve information quality	• Decision support system • Options to filter and organize information

Figure 8–4
Knowledge Innovation Factors and Personas

- *Process factors.* Tasks and work processes that are performed as the primary activity need a variety of information provided to support their successful completion. The format, presentation, filtering, organization, and summary of information must match the context of the individual users.
- *Social factors.* It is important to establish communities of widely dispersed individuals, customers, suppliers, and partners to interact with product and services teams in the firm. They come together to capture, share, and exchange knowledge for the purpose of meeting their assigned goals and objectives.
- *Relationship factors.* To design the intended experience, managers should create a composite of information technology, application, and c-commerce capabilities. Details should be provided about the integration of these capabilities to make the user experience easy to understand and engage within. The fact that several applications, information sources, and other software features are working together will be transparent to the individual users.

REPUTATION—FROM INDIVIDUAL TO NETWORK

In the past, firms would base their reputation on physical interactions between individuals within the organization and those outside the organization. The public relations and corporate communications departments managed most of internal and external formal communications. In the c-commerce firm of the future, customer relationships and partnerships will become the cornerstone of the organization. Control of information about individuals and the firm will be much more decentralized and available from sources published throughout the Internet and intranet.

Relationship networks are distributed unevenly in organizations. People who work together form direct network relationships. Project teams build direct relationships. Functional business areas build direct relationships. On these teams, everyone knows everyone else with only a few individuals who are tied to other teams, forming indirect relationships. If these indirect relationships are infrequent and weak, then information and knowledge will not flow quickly and will not be available throughout the organization.

In most cases, the knowledge needed is in external teams and firms. Relationship networks have a horizon beyond which it is difficult to see what is happening. A clear picture of information is available from direct contacts and their direct contacts. Information outside this will not be available or it will be unclear. Basically, teams are blind to what is happening in the rest of the network, with the exception of public information, which is known by everyone. The optimal situation is to have employees separated from each other and from management by only two or three relationships or conversations; this enables access to accurate information and a good understanding of the firm's structure and operation.

TRUST—FROM POWER TO KNOWLEDGE

Trust in the traditional firm lies in believing and supporting the decisions made by executive leaders. It is a power structure, and employees either trust the organization and its decisions or they don't. C-commerce expands the boundaries of the firm to include suppliers, partners, and customers and includes them on virtual teams working to meet identified goals and objectives. Trust can no longer be centralized in a few decision makers and will have to expand across many firms and decision makers. We have to trust the information available and believe in the partnerships established across the value chain.

There are two activities that need to be completed early in identifying and defining work processes. The first is to identify and include the key stakeholders in the work process program. The second is to begin building relationships with individuals in key roles of the work process. Most firms pay a great deal of attention to designing enterprise work processes, but many firms neglect or mishandle the relationship-building activities. Establishing great relationships will do a lot more to build trust and ensure success than a well-written work process diagram. Several fallacies contribute to the thinking that makes managers pay more attention to the work process design than to relationships. Consider the following:

- The key to a successful work process and c-commerce initiative is writing a good work process design. The reality is that the work process design is not a working document.

It is used to outline expectations for everyone involved in targeted work processes. For employees, the work process design is used to gain alignment for the work process and c-commerce initiative. From that point forward the people, processes, and information will continue to evolve. The work process design will not ensure that process management and relationship management are successful.

- Relationship building begins after the work process is designed. This is false; if the work process design has been completed by a self-contained team, it will be difficult to shift to a collaborative format. It is never too early to establish the fundamentals of a good working relationship. Progress made on relationship development during work process design will benefit and help ensure successful relationship management in the future.

COMMERCE—FROM TRANSACTIONAL AND OPERATIONAL TO GROWTH and LEARNING

Within an individual firm, the interchange of ideas is frequently focused on both transactional and operational activities. Moving toward c-commerce, individuals within the organization will have to know more about how their transactional and operational activities interrelate to other business units, suppliers, customers, and partners throughout the supply chain to provide the knowledge needs for growth and learning. Network maps provide a revealing snapshot of the work processes at a particular point in time. These maps can help answer many key questions in the relationship-building process.

- Who is playing a leadership role in the work process? Who is not, but should be?
- Are indirect relationships developing around key customer issues?
- Who are the work process experts?
- Who are the mentors that others look to for advice?
- Who are the innovators? Are ideas shared and acted on?
- Are collaborative activities and projects forming between cross-functional team members and functions?

- What measurements will be focused on to provide results around the primary business driver for individuals, teams, functions, and customers?
- Are the right relationships in place? Are any key relationships missing?

Before the relationship network can be improved, an assessment of the current situation needs to be completed. The goal is to design strategies to create new relationships. The transformation the firm will experience is the result of many interchanges of ideas throughout the relationship network. The c-commerce transformation can be guided by understanding and catalyzing connections. For example, knowledge of where connections exist and where they need to be created allows a relationship management office to influence local interactions. If the relationship and human networks are known, influence can be focused. Consider the following:

- Team members with better access to individuals inside and outside the organization finish their assignments faster.
- Team members with better connections discover and transfer the knowledge they need within the organization.
- Leaders with better connections inside and outside the organization identify and develop more opportunities for their team or firm.
- Process owners with better network connections are more successful achieving business driver goals.

TRANSPARENCY—FROM SIX DEGREES OF SEPARATION TO TWO DEGREES OF SEPARATION

In a network with many degrees of separation between relationships and their frequency of communication, the ability to find knowledge or information needed is constrained. If the knowledge being searched for is not within the known relationship network, then employees assume it is not available in the firm and it is reinvented or purchased. Why not use the power of the relationship networks to create another solution? Create a relationship management office or function to improve the organizational network and then use technology to help people communicate across global teams. Begin looking at the core work processes and the primary business driver to identify how the firm is organized around a specific topic, product, service, or customer. Use social network analysis techniques to create a map of current relationship networks and begin to focus on improving the flow or exchange of knowledge.

Traditionally, firms have paid little attention to the relationship networks that exist internally, externally, or in the community. Things have changed over the past decade. Now, with the help of resources such as the Internet and personal information devices, we have access to everyone in the world. (Some say we are separated by six or fewer relationships.) In other words, I would be able to arrange an introduction to the chief executive at IBM by working with people in my relationship network and it will take six or fewer contacts throughout our networks to find someone who can connect me. It might take many more than six conversations to identify these six or fewer relationships. C-commerce, with some help from technology, creates an integrated and adaptive relationship network throughout the supply chain in which any person can find what he or she is looking for through just one or two relationships. These nurtured and well-managed relationship networks will allow communication, knowledge, and learning to transparently move through the supply chain. Firms such as Visible Path are creating people connections for business processes, and firms such as Cisco are experimenting with social networking and relationship capital collaboration solutions.

Networks—From Business Units and Functional Teams to Business Processes and Virtual Teams

Firms currently rely on people working in business units and functional teams to produce shareholder value and customer satisfaction. C-commerce requires that virtual teams work together to accomplish core business processes across the supply chain. Over time, individuals will identify with several communities, teams, or clusters of people that they work with and have less personal accountability and identification with the reporting structure of the firm. A complex network of connections drives c-commerce. All individuals, communities, systems, and work processes are interconnected. To meet our objectives, we need to manage our connected assets and individual performance. Research on productivity and effectiveness provides lessons learned into what works in the connected supply chain. The value of contacts (relationship capital) is becoming more important than knowledge (human capital). We have found success stories of executives who are significantly better at accomplishing their objectives through relationships than their co-workers. Human capital and relationship capital working together create both innovation and improvement.

Effective leaders have to reach a diverse set of people in their network through very few connections to be extremely successful. Individuals who use people who are directly tied to their project or objectives to seek and find information are quickly overwhelmed with too many connections. Successful individuals limit the number of direct relationships they manage and connect with individuals who have an indirect relationship to their objectives to get what they need in the shortest amount of time. Team members need to have relationships to others outside the team for benefits and opportunities to be maximized. These diverse relationship networks with many unique indirect connections are good for monitoring what is happening in the organization and for discovering pockets of knowledge and expertise.

The work process and c-commerce initiative will require a landscape of technologies to provide the capabilities needed to share explicit knowledge that can be captured, documented, and transferred indirectly through the firm. The complex tacit knowledge throughout the firm will require direct interaction and sharing of experiences between two or more individuals. To transfer tacit knowledge, a direct connection with the knowledge sources must be established. It is the trust and understanding that develops over time that becomes the foundation for knowledge to be shared and learned.

BOUNDARIES—FROM FORMAL AND PHYSICAL TO INFORMAL AND VIRTUAL

In today's firms, individual accountabilities and responsibilities can be clearly defined through formal reporting structures and physical locations. In the future, as systems become open and integrated, there will be multiple reporting structures that people will be accountable for managing. Virtual, global, and dynamic teams will define how work is completed. Process owners, process providers, service providers, and customer support teams need to understand the domain of knowledge their groups represent. When team members do not understand the roles of individuals, teams, and functions involved in virtual teams, the motivation level of all team members is reduced; team members will not be clear on who provides opinions and decisions, when to provide their input and opinions, and what their comments represent. Process team leaders will require a clear understanding of work processes, why work processes are managed globally, and how they can be effective in leading virtual teams. For example, virtual team members might be required to perform the same roles and responsibilities and service the local customer. Based on their responsibilities they could be focused on products and services that cross geographical borders. These distinctions need to be understood by everyone working on the virtual team. The following are two important factors related to virtual teams:

- Think globally and understand the benefits. Not all work processes require diverse perspectives, specialized team members, or flexible locations to manage customer and service agreements. When a virtual team is required to meet the objectives of the work process activities and deliverables, the team needs to be chartered and process team leads assigned.
- Clarity around roles and responsibilities is key. Prepare a matrix of the skills and knowledge domains that will need to be represented on the virtual teams. The list of skills is approved by the process owner. The process team leaders are selected and the team members are added based on the human capital and relationship capital needed to successfully complete the activities and objectives of the work process. The virtual team will be managed using the experience designed through interactive c-commerce technologies.

REAL-TIME COLLABORATION ENTERPRISE—FROM SINGLE DIMENSIONAL TO MULTIDIMENSIONAL

People rely on collaboration capabilities that are available as tools or independent applications within their IT landscape. Teams frequently look for one or two applications that will meet their immediate needs. C-commerce will focus on the multiple dimensions built into how individuals, teams, and networks interact and complete processes. The IT landscape will integrate enterprise capabilities into how people work.

Virtual teams will be working together to meet defined work process and c-commerce objectives. Earlier in the chapter we described the contacts that would need to be established to build the relationship network. The focus here is to describe in more detail what needs to be done to make the individual connections and relationships successful. In many cases individuals and team members will be spread across the globe working collaboratively to complete assigned activities with minimal or no face-to-face interaction.

Building effective relationships with global team members will require incorporating a few new best practices. Additional focus needs to be given to communications; essentially all interactions will be completed through Web-based applications, the Internet, and the extranet. Everyone will need to have some cultural awareness because English will be a second language in many cases. There also will be differences in expertise and difficulties understanding how individuals with different backgrounds will interpret conversations and interactions. Sharing work processes will require additional clarity around team objectives and the actual outcomes anticipated.

Compile information about team members' activities that are challenging and highly interdependent across the work process. Develop thoughts on how to deal with the diversity of the team and the degree of virtual or electronic work team members will need to complete. The differences between procedural, heuristic, and executive work will be described when the work is shared across multiple functions or multiple firms in several time zones. The goal is to provide information that will assist employees and managers in practices that build team cohesiveness, trust, and shared understanding.

Governance—From Resource Management to Partnership Management

In a traditional firm, portfolio management and resource management drive what is going to be done and who is going to do it. The c-commerce organization of the future will be driven first through partnership management of virtual teams; then, individual firms in the value chain will be able to define and execute their portfolio management and resource management plans. Several policies are needed to successfully enable virtual process teams. These policies provide the structure leaders need to help team members work effectively in formal reporting relationships and informal reporting relationships. Leaders need to know how to intervene immediately when problems associated with working as a virtual team arise. Policies will give employees the necessary focus on team objectives and deemphasize individual success. Other policies encourage leaders and team members to work with c-commerce technologies and begin to envision what the virtual working world looks like and understand what is expected of everyone. A link to performance appraisals will ensure that the goals and objectives of the work process and c-commerce are incorporated by every leader and employee. The following are key governance requirements for an organization instituting c-commerce:

- Dedicated team leaders are vital. Leaders of process providers, service providers, and customer support teams need to allocate a significant portion of their time to communicating frequently and regularly with each individual team member. These conversations cover a variety of topics beyond clarification of current tasks, including any personal concerns. Performance of assigned tasks and objectives and plans for career development and mentoring need to be discussed on a regular basis. Contributions to knowledge repositories and interactive c-commerce technology best practices should be reviewed in these individual discussions. Team leaders will have additional responsibilities to manage virtual meetings, events, process changes, communications, and other shared systems, technologies, and information sources to make teamwork more effective.

- Performance appraisals should include virtual process team objectives. Virtual team members will frequently have multiple reporting relationships. They will report into the hierarchical organization through a local manager and have additional responsibilities and tasks to complete as part of this team. The local manager will usually be responsible for completing performance appraisal activities and deliverables. The process team leader needs to provide quarterly updates in a formal presentation using the interactive c-commerce technologies for broad awareness of work process accomplishments and ongoing action plans. In addition, the process team leader will need to work closely with the local manager to include work process objectives, measurement, and progress updates that will be incorporated into individual team member performance appraisals.
- Human capital and relationship capital are as important as meeting work process and other objectives. Each person will have objectives and measurements included in his or her performance appraisal for high priority work process and functional responsibilities. The activities and objectives to improve communication and share knowledge with contacts (relationship capital) and the career development objectives outlined to improve knowledge (human capital) need to be included in individual performance appraisals. The firm's investment in relationship capital and human capital will define its competitive advantage and differentiate the firm from competitors. The capability to learn, adapt to change, and innovate to create new products and services is critical for continued growth in the marketplace and as an organization; these capabilities are achieved through continuous improvement of relationship capital and human capital throughout the organization.
- Business value for travel is justified as part of the approval process. Working virtually requires individuals, teams, functions, suppliers, partners, and customers to use different skills than are used when working face-to-face. Process team leaders will have to outline the c-commerce experience with the following steps: (1) develop an experience positioning as the main storyline and a value promise that describes the desired experience; (2) create an experience specification that describes how c-commerce capabilities

will be used to create the desired experience; and (3) create an experience design that describes the changes in relationships, roles, and environmental elements that influence the user experience. Once the c-commerce experience is established, travel will be limited to business value that cannot be met through the virtual working environment.

- Interactive c-commerce technologies should be established and shared among users in the relationship network. The virtual process team will require the use of technologies that can be used by everyone working on the process. These are the interactive c-commerce capabilities that will be shared by virtual team members to seamlessly work across multiple time zones, languages, and other differences. Continue to refine the c-commerce experience throughout the supply chain for participants. Build how individuals, teams, functions, and customers are expected to interact within the c-commerce experience into processes and other organization changes that might be needed. Make sure that users have the knowledge, skills, and tools to interact with people, processes, and information. Process team leaders will be required to institute management practices that measure, reinforce, and improve the experience.
- Work process and c-commerce governance should be structured as an interactive virtual team. Process teams and relationship networks will be executing within the firm. Most individuals, teams, and functions have experience working in traditional hierarchical reporting structures. These formal reporting structures will have to blend into a collection of informal reporting relationships. This means that individuals will have multiple bosses that come from different functions or departments within the organization. It is important that the local managers, process owners, and process team leaders work with individuals through any conflicts, priorities, and other miscommunications that occur over time. Having management, governance teams, and interactive virtual teams using the same c-commerce experience for their interactions will accelerate resolving issues and concerns, improving communications, and implementing change.

GUIDELINES FOR TRANSITIONING TO C-COMMERCE

Leaders and managers in the firm that are driving c-commerce into business processes will need to establish a collection of guidelines to help employees, suppliers, customers, and partners through the transition. Several guidelines are included here for consideration. Every firm's best practices will be unique and designed specifically around the behaviors that are targeted for change.

Design Relationship Management into Work Processes

Once core work processes have been identified, there will be several months of work before the first phase of the initiative is implemented. This is the time to get process owners, leadership, and delivery teams working together. Key players work together to identify business drivers, core processes, performance measurements, and c-commerce capabilities. In addition, they need to successfully execute process management and relationship management once the details are worked through. It is critical to identify the cultural issues and to agree on common principles on which relationships will operate. We recommend first concentrating on developing a set of principles to guide and govern the relationships needed. Some companies have used professional facilitators who understand both process-building and relationship-building steps. These experts bring an understanding of what needs to done and how it needs to be done to accelerate designing work processes and building relationships as part of the effort.

Assign the Same Team to Design Processes and Manage Relationships

One of the biggest mistakes managers make when instituting c-commerce is not having the key players work together to identify business drivers, core processes, and performance measurements; this causes c-commerce capabilities to overlap, with the process owners and other team members managing the relationship after the fact. The key players need to be accountable and made to live with the results of their efforts. The process owners and future team members need to be grounded in the context of the work done by the implementation team. This will help them understand the underlying motivations behind the business case and avoid pursuing goals they do not understand. Make certain that members of the implementation team continue as process owners and future team members. Complete a well-structured knowledge transfer plan to avoid a long and unnecessary familiarization phase.

Focus on Knowledge-Transfer Activities

Successful execution of the work process and c-commerce initiative requires a great deal of knowledge sharing and transfer between the customer and work processes. Customers bring a deep understanding of their needs and expectations. They have valuable market and industry know-how and a strong familiarity with the organization's culture and context. The customer will ultimately drive how decisions are really made and how work really gets done. The informal relationship networks need to understand the customer as part of their tacit knowledge. Some of this knowledge will be embedded into procedures, applications, and products that will need to be transferred through formal and informal relationship networks.

The firm needs to identify and understand the tacit and explicit knowledge required to create an effective working relationship with customers and then put the appropriate transfer mechanisms in place. For example, training and orientation workshops can help to facilitate the transfer of formal expertise and explicit knowledge. Establishing mentoring relationships and assigning partners can enable the transfer of tacit knowledge.

Manage Virtual Teams

The key to the virtual team's success is its ability to take advantage of the differences among members. Virtual teams are established to bring together a variety of people with different knowledge, roles, and constituents to meet customer needs. The following are guidelines for helping team members understand and appreciate their differences.

- *Identify differences.* The virtual team members will need to learn about each other's work styles, preferences, cultural backgrounds, country norms, personal experiences, and past accomplishments. Shared experiences will be electronic. It is important to use the Internet and other c-commerce and learning technologies to begin the team's experiences working in this format. Forming activities are critical to use as reference points to make future decisions and work through issues as they arise.
- *Establish shared group norms.* Virtual team norms will revolve around scheduled activities, meetings, and other collaboration protocols. There are several ideas to consider. Meeting formats can include time in the agenda for individual opinions to be shared without comment from other team members. Team meetings are scheduled for different times to accommodate the different time zones and will encourage team members to share inconveniences and stay focused on the agenda. Team members will share a calendar that tells when individuals are working and how they can be reached. Standards and best practices around e-mail, shared document libraries, how frequently to review the team Web site, and other details will be agreed on by team members.
- *Create common procedures.* Virtual teams will need to establish a shared set of procedures. They need to integrate local work practices with those of other team members to ease communication, understanding, and sharing of resources. Successful virtual teams have established a common set of work practices and procedures that came about by integrating best practices from their different locations or using already established firmwide procedures.
- *Hold frequent team virtual conferences.* Process team leaders will need to hold frequent team virtual conferences. It is important that all team members attend these meetings. These are structured meetings for discussion of how activities are distributed among the team members, report-

ing on status, how deliverables and activities are coordinated, and discussions. These discussions are critical to make certain team members understand how individual activities, deliverables, and issues are affecting everyone. Issues are then discussed in more detail.

- *Redistribute activities among team members frequently.* To realize the benefits of relationship capital and human capital, it is important that team members share knowledge. It turns out that this is best done when specific activities have to be accomplished. Process team leaders will often assign pairs of individuals to complete tasks in which one team member will benefit significantly by learning from the other. Once the activity is successfully completed the individual team members will move onto new tasks and activities.

- *Stress energizing activities.* Virtual teams, more than teams that are located physically together, can lose their sense of purpose, shared identity, and excitement. Meetings to enhance team cohesiveness can be held at any time, for any reason. Hold strategy sessions, team development sessions, and lessons-learned sessions to energize the team. The format for energizing activities will depend on the depth and breadth of these sessions. They can be facilitated as virtual conferences or face-to-face. If a several-day event were to be planned, getting together in person would be beneficial.

Volvo—Supply Chain Collaboration Case Summary

Volvo has developed a best practice of challenging and fusing ideas and capabilities of a geographically dispersed team and quickly converting concepts into products by bringing greater clarity into the innovation process. The company has developed a best practice called the Innovation Management Center, which features three levels—executive portfolio management, project management, and end-user collaboration. Team members can work with design-chain partners to brainstorm, define, and validate product possibilities, review concepts, and ultimately present new product concepts to executives. Project managers can easily track and monitor activities and deliverables, and executives can manage their product development portfolio.

This environment parallels the physical world of war rooms and project rooms and facilitates the creation of more unique and innovative product possibilities, which are then defined, explored, and ultimately validated. This enables manufacturers and their supplier networks to increase new product successes by 200% through harvesting, testing, and converting more raw ideas into market-dominating products, ensuring the development of more innovative products within critical windows of opportunity (Groves & Chris 2002).

According to Benny Sommerfield, Volvo's innovation concept business manager, the new collaborative project environment supporting team ability to review concepts in the context of new product programs and executives has helped to streamline business processes and increase capacity for throughput. With the Innovation Management Center, Volvo has been able to significantly decrease the concept cycle time, allowing for more focus on the upstream innovation process requirements.

McKinsey

McKinsey, the international strategy firm, has done something quite remarkable. When an employee joins McKinsey, he or she becomes a permanent source of relationship capital to the McKinsey family. A database of all current and former McKinsey employees is accessible to all McKinsey employees. Employees can search the company's database and determine a multitude of important relationships that can be leveraged in every Fortune 500 engagement they may be involved in. In some offices they go as far as to market their alumni to top headhunters. Typically, McKinsey partners who have left the firm move into very senior executive positions. It's a powerful network available to McKinsey employees.

Few organizations have developed such a powerful network relationship ecosystem to support their continued conversations for sustaining growth in business. A program such as this starts with the strategic vision that an organization is nothing without its talent, regardless of the cultures and companies it is located in. Each network is a door to a future business possibility. The network grows in depth of experience and breadth of relationships as individuals throughout the network continue to share experiences and establish new and deeper relationships. The magic is creating a communication context to continue to share, learn, and grow using the mutual reciprocity exchanges throughout the global network. Companies that have achieved a combined work process, collaboration, and relationship network are some of the most powerful, agile, and flexible that we have researched.

Linked In—A Social Networking Business Model

Linked In, a Palo Alto, Calif., company founded in 2003, has developed a c-commerce business model centered on social capital principles. The company is a network of professionals who help each other reconnect with past colleages or generate new networks for growth and problem solving. Who uses Linked In? To date, the service is primarily used by recruiters, investment professionals, management consultants, analysts, and market researchers. The stickiness uptake is very high, with more than 84% of requests for contacts being fulfilled. The solution helps strengthen relationship ties by providing endorsements of character and talent.

The company has received more than $5 million in venture capital by leading investors including Sequoia Capital and Greylock Capital. Linked In has already demonstrated rapid growth, going from an early launch of fewer than 10,000 members to having more than 3.4 million members in August 2005, and expanding its base by 250,000 new members monthly. The solution spans geographies, with a market mix of more than 1.7 million North American members, 1 million Europeans, and the rest in Asia and Latin America. A professional joins Linked In every 10 seconds, and more than 400,000 Linked In users are chief executives or executive management. Linked In has a business model that is focused on enabling relationship connections. Here is a business model with no marketing budget or sales staff, yet every morning new customers become members. The growth is driven much like Google, eBay, and Hotmail, where power is placed in the hands of networks to connect and add value.

In a recent interview with founder Konstantin Guericke, he shared some of the key trends in social networking. "In today's business economy, people have limited time and need to secure the strongest business relationships possible. Having access to referrals that are reputation based from other networks improves the insight, and judgments are formed more rapidly. Leveraging the collective intelligence where social capital filters information transforms into a competitive advantage. The Internet is a transformation highway, which easily accelerates and increases the visibility of information. Reputation management is becoming more and more important for business effectiveness and career success."

Interview with Konstantin Guericke, Linked In founder, Aug. 19, 2005.

CONCLUSION

Managers need to understand the available skills and competencies throughout the firm and how they are used for competitive advantage across the industry value chain. Knowing how they are used to accomplish operational and strategic objectives is also important. There are several key relationships and personas that will have been identified that can be used to design, orchestrate, and capitalize on relationship network experiences. This is the foundation of the firm's social nexus and begins to define the current and future value of relationship networks in the organization.

Who we know (relationship capital) is frequently more important than what we know (human capital). C-commerce allows us to capitalize on and maximize the combined human capital and relationship capital to create both innovation and improvement. Using c-commerce capabilities to help employees learn, adapt to change, and improve innovation will set the organization apart from competitors. In terms of an internal focus, c-commerce benefits continuous improvement efforts in the areas of relationship capital and human capital throughout the firm.

Chapter 9 introduces culture and change as they relate to the ten c-commerce capabilities. Organizational cultures are moving from uniformity to diversity. For the past century, business models have been managed by countless policies and procedures in which employees are rewarded for loyalty to the firm. Business dynamics are forcing more distributed decision making supported by global, project-based, and diverse cultures that need shared c-commerce solutions, goals, and objectives.

9

THE CULTURE AND CHANGE DIMENSION

Culture is the sum of socially transmitted behavior patterns, arts, beliefs, rituals, artifacts, institutions, and all other products of human work and thought. To put it more simply: Culture involves what people think, what they do, and what material products they produce. Culture also has several collaborative properties: It is shared, symbolic, transmitted across generations, adaptive, and integrated.

Margaret Mead once said, "Never doubt that a small group of thoughtful, committed citizens can change the world; indeed it is the only thing that ever has." Mead recognized that innovation and change begin with a few people who believe that there is a better way to live. Executives and leaders understand that a shift to a major global support economy is well under way; however, there is much cultural work to be done to develop stronger collaboration and transparency capabilities.

How chief executives choose to develop collaborative organizational cultures with reflection and renewal capabilities will determine organizations' ability to survive. Culture and change are at the heart of c-commerce development; the process is part of a digital evolution moving us closer to realizing and tapping into unused skills and talents of people. The toughest challenge

Governance

	Traditional Approach	C-Commerce Approach
⊃ Strategy	Firm First	Customer First
⊃ Process	Hierarchical Ownership	Distributed Ownership
⊃ IT	Closed and Proprietary	Open and Standards
⊃ People	Resource Management	Partnership Management
⊃ **Culture**	Prescriptive	Self-Regulating
⊃ Measurement	Firm Shareholder	Value Chain Shareholders

Figure 9–1
Culture Dimensions

facing organizations is to successfully design and execute collaborative cultures. Can fundamental c-commerce changes in leadership style or organizational culture be achieved? Scientific studies show the odds are nine to one against success (Deutschman 2005). Most organizations today conduct employee satisfaction surveys annually and, year after year, results indicate that employee trust in leadership is eroding rapidly. Too many managers have a credibility and trust gap with the people they are managing. Credibility is based on perceptions of trustworthiness, reliability, and integrity. According to Bruce Katcher, president of Discovery Surveys, a Massachusetts-based firm specializing in conducting employee opinion and customer satisfaction surveys, less than 53% of employees believe the information they receive from senior management. He based his estimates on a review of the company's database of more than 30,000 respondents from 44 international companies. Unfortunately, the development of collaborative, trusting cultures is not happening fast enough to counter this continued erosion in employee and customer confidence.

This chapter provides a comprehensive review of collaboration culture attributes and examples of companies applying collaboration culture fundamentals to achieve new ways of working. In preparing to align organizational culture with a c-commerce business strategy, understanding where the organi-

Culture and Change

	Traditional Approach	C-Commerce Approach
⊃ **Purpose**	Uniformity	Diversity
⊃ **Identity**	Singular	Plural
⊃ **Reputation**	Narrow	Comprehensive
⊃ **Trust**	Selective	Inclusive
⊃ **Commerce**	Transactional	Partnering
⊃ **Transparency**	Conflict Orientation	Constructive Orientation
⊃ **Networks**	Few and Long-Term	Many and Volatile
⊃ **Boundaries**	Rigid and solid	Fluid and Porous
⊃ **Real-Time Collaboration**	Cautious and Methodical	Curious and Adaptive
⊃ **Governance**	Prescriptive	Self-Regulating

Figure 9–2
Culture and Change and Collaboration

zation's culture is starting from is an important planning requirement. Figure 9–2 summarizes the major attributes defining organizational culture within the context of c-commerce.

PURPOSE—FROM UNIFORMITY TO DIVERSITY

For the past century, organizational cultures have developed
business models that run like clocks; these cultures can be characterized as mechanical, rigid, process centric, and with countless rules and procedures. Employees traditionally have been
rewarded for loyalty to the firm. These cultural rituals helped
create uniform behaviors. Today, hierarchical and uniform cultures remain pervasive worldwide, but many firms are striving
to evolve from rigid, uniform, and hierarchical operating models
to more fluid, project-based, and diverse cultures.

For a firm to successfully compete in the collaboration and
support economy and develop corporate cultures that have a
deep collaborative purpose, the core business foundation must
be based on diversity. Diversity is best defined as inclusive

dimensions of gender, skill, thought, belief, and desires. The world has become far too complex to demand conformity of talent to fit into a cultural behavioral pattern. Understanding cultures that are undergoing rapid economic growth is critical to business success. For example, in less than 7 years, more than 95% of the Internet pages will be written in Chinese, Hindi, or Arabic (Bontis 2005). The inability to absorb the knowledge of Chinese, Indian, and Arabic business cultures could have catastrophic implications for a firm's growth prospects.

Firms that continue to reinforce rigid cultures with behaviors that are inconsistent in practice and action will be obsolete in the next century. They simply will not have the organizational cultural elasticity to adapt to change. To secure strong diversity capabilities, chief executives will need to strengthen their organization's core cultural competencies in divergent thinking, trust making, knowledge sharing, partnering, and leadership comfort to work effectively within constantly changing boundaries.

Identity—From Singular to Pluralism

When it comes to cultural identity, organizations in the Western world have traditionally looked at developing cultures with a focus on what it means to be an employee in a firm. Organizations carefully craft corporate vision statements and departmental mission statements and establish a value system in an attempt to achieve cultural assimilation more rapidly. In the past, these practices have worked well, and today they remain common business practices. The reality, unfortunately, is that organizational identities have many subcultures, often resulting from mergers and acquisitions, and can vary significantly among functional areas and regions. Organizations that seriously embrace creating strong collaborative identities in their culture will learn how to move from a singular cultural identify to a plural cultural identity. Some of the ways organizations can start their transition from singular to plural identity are summarized.

- Understand that cultural diversity and multiple identities are to be embraced. Don't be afraid of chaos; patterns will emerge when guiding principles, as opposed to rigid operating procedures, are implemented.

- Ensure that cultural anthropologists are recruited into senior executive positions in the organization. They have rich insights into cultural behaviors; skills to identify the organization's narrative patterns, rituals, and hidden socialization patterns (that are not documented); and can help outline cultural identity as a competitive brand differentiator.
- Recognize the value of integrated design competencies in developing diversity; the customer experience has become more important than the product. Merging creative design and packaging and consumer experience experts with expertise in areas such as rapid prototype design, creative drawing and visualization, branding, and color is becoming increasingly important.
- Strive to ensure that the board of directors and executives leading the organization mirror the reality of a global cultural landscape and the customer base.

To migrate from singular to plural identity, managers must identify and understand the organization's cultural patterns and rituals. One effective way to get started is to strive to adopt new performance management practices that integrate the individual view as a starting point and move into building the corporate view. This approach fosters collaborative cultures based on the core competency of trust. Trust will grow and be nurtured as employees become fully engaged and challenged in their work.

The Total Performance Scorecard (TPS) system developed by Dr. Hubert Rampersad promotes a new management approach. It attempts to maximize personal development of all corporate employees or associates by optimizing the use of their capabilities, thereby improving organizational performance. This approach differs substantially from traditional management concepts. An important difference is that TPS uses personal mission and vision as the starting point. Traditional improvement and change management concepts incorporate learning but rarely take into account the specific personal ambitions of employees. As a consequence, superficial improvements are made while trust and commitment to the firm do not improve or continue to decline. TPS has proven that personal involvement stimulates individual and team learning, creativity, and self-motivation. If personal ambition is the starting point, people will cooperate with more dedication, which inspires motivation, trust, and commitment.

Moving from cultural foundations of singularity to pluralism is a key to developing stronger diversity and c-commerce competencies. Practical approaches like the Total Performance Scorecard system are being used in pioneering organizations such as Shell, ABN, Amro, and Lucent. As executives wake up to the power of bringing the total person to work and organizational performance improves, stronger pluralism competencies will evolve.

REPUTATION—FROM NARROW TO COMPREHENSIVE

A collaboration economy expands the importance of reputation. Because of the rapidly emerging Internet economy, an individual's reputation is visible and transparent. New generations of software tools have emerged to support connectivity and collaboration needs. These new tools are called social networking and collaborating tools and have spawned numerous companies including Linked In, Orkut, Groove, Ryze, Friendster, Tribe Network, Tickle, Zero Degrees, and Match.com. These companies are rapidly proving that social connectivity and collaborative solutions can assist an organization's growth. The value proposition is simple: A company with thousands of workers could have millions of contacts. But making these contacts useful requires being able to identify the right one at the right time. The social network data is spread across e-mail servers, contact files, and customer relationship management or sales-force automation systems. By crawling and cataloging these systems, firms can identify and take advantage of their social networks.

How well a contact is known creates a reputation-profiling attribute to identify the strength of relationships. For example, Visible Path takes into account everything from the number of e-mails two people exchange to how often they appear in the "cc:" line instead of the "to:" line. If there are several relationship paths connecting a user to a contact, each is ranked by strength. This type of information is used in recruiting, business development, and sales processes. In a survey of senior executives by the University of North Carolina, 84% of respondents said they would always or usually take a sales call from someone a colleague referred, and only 8% said they would usually take a call from a total stranger.

Reputations are being leveraged in blogs, wikis, and social networking software solutions on the Internet. Google can count an individual's reputation profile links. The count reflects how many times a person's name is mentioned throughout all Web-based pages on the Internet. The result is a derived reputation value in terms of influence reach. Firms such as Spoke and Visible Path are integrating six degrees of separation, social networking software analytics to help optimize networking of people-to-people connections for c-commerce interactions. Spoke says that prioritizing sales leads according to the strength of relationships resulted in a 35% increase in lead pickup for one client, and sales were closed 2.5 times as often.

Developing cultures where reputation has been harvested will be critical for organizations to compete in the next century. Moving forward, chief executives will strive to make sense of c-commerce and embrace social networking solutions to create more open and transparent cultures. They will be able to build relationships and reputations to derive value. The payback will be enormous.

TRUST—FROM SELECTIVE TO INCLUSIVE

Employee trust is fundamental to an organization's success. While the bottom line will continue to be important, organizations that focus only on shareholder value and profitability will ultimately lose both. Dee Hock, founder and CEO emeritus of Visa, argues, "Making money is not a purpose, though it may be a necessity." In addition to making money, firms need to reduce conflict, increase collaboration, replace polarization with understanding and consensus, and mobilize people to work toward common goals. Key principles that firms should focus on when striving to develop strong, inclusive, trusting cultures include the following:

- Trust is earned over time. An employee's history of conversation and experiences determines his or her level of reciprocity and generates good will. Cultures that develop effective collaboration practices are in fact practicing learning conversations or telling narrative stories. The most important conversations that are happening in the organization are not happening in training rooms, conference rooms, or boardrooms, but rather in cafeterias and office cubicle doorways. As employees exchange their know-how via phone conversations, e-mail exchanges, and meeting conversations, they are sharing critical business knowledge, exploring underlying assumptions, and creating solutions to key business issues. Imagine that the office grapevine is really a reflective mirror of the vitality and richness of the organization's cultural workings. Imagine that the branching and intertwining vines are the natural ecosystems supporting knowledge, information, and energy flows. The more trust earned, the more sap pours through the vines, and the more growth, creativity, and innovation can be harvested.

- Trust is embedded in conversations. Dr. David Isaac, in researching dialogue (2003), asked hundreds of executives and employees in diverse cultures around the world what qualities of a conversation make it worthwhile. Responses included the following:
  - Trust in conversations is enriched when there is a sense of mutual respect.
  - Taking the time to really talk together, and reflect about what we each thought, is important.
  - We listened to each other, even if there were major differences.
  - I was accepted and not judged by the others in the conversation.
  - The conversation helped to strengthen our relationship.
  - We explored questions that really mattered.
  - We developed shared meaning that wasn't there when we began.
  - I learned something new or important.
  - It strengthened our mutual commitment.

- For firms to create trust, they will need to develop conversation as a core business process practice. Fernando Flores, one of the first researchers to define the value of conversation competency, said, "An organization's results are determined through the webs of human commitments, born in webs of human conversations" (Hughes 2004). Humans share a common heritage as social beings; together in conversation, they organize for action and create a common future.

- Trust can be monitored. Developing trust as a core business competency will happen through healthy dialogue and enriching conversations at all levels throughout the firm. Over time trust will grow and improve as reputation and social networking evolves.
- There have been trust emergences in community networks. Blogs, wikis, and relationship networks are examples of technologies used to build trust in communities. Consider the following:
  - *Web logs (blogs).* This capability allows an individual to post short, informal dialogues organized in distributed conversations of rolling lists that are unedited and used for communication. These informal logs add relevant and interesting commentary throughout the team. If facilitated correctly, the content is compelling and drives traffic and repeat visitors to the blog Web site. When focused on work processes, people can produce high-quality, focused blogs to provide innovation, ideas, and support throughout the community of suppliers, customers, partners, and team members.
  - *Wikis.* This capability is an asynchronous collaborative Web site where suppliers, customers, partners, and other team members are all authors. Anyone can edit, delete, or modify all content. A facilitator is assigned to manage and enforce best practices. Wikis are used as a composition system, discussion medium, and repository, and are a tool for collaboration that provides users with a common structure and vocabulary to discuss their work processes, accomplishments, and objectives.
  - *Dynamic creation of relationship networks to inform and connect people.* This is the ability to find individuals throughout the enterprise (employees, customers, suppliers, and partners) related to the work process, activities, or topic being addressed. This capability can be used to dynamically locate subject matter experts and include them as needed to meet defined objectives.

Table 9–1 *High-Trust Collaborating Cultures vs. Low-Trust Collaborating Cultures*

High-Trust Behaviors	Low-Trust Behaviors
Authentic, transparent, open	Frequent behavior changes (chameleon), closed
Supportive, respectful, honest	Backbiting, blaming, accusing, disrespectful
Nurturing and flexible	Controlling and rigid
Servant leadership; empowering and self-supervision	Controlling, monitoring, rules and regulations, spying
Trust and high integrity	Distrust and low integrity
Proactive, performance orientation	Reactive, changing expectations
Freedom to explore, learn, and grow	Strict protocols, regulated environment, learning by status
Learning culture, risk taking, reflection and renewal	Transferring blame, risk adversity, fear of repercussions
Loyalty, accountability, empowerment	Lack of accountability, "travel in packs," political and fear based
Ethical and open	Red tape and closed
Self-managed virtual teams	Large groups of staff under tight, controlled supervision
Positive, fun, and learning atmosphere	Negative, joyless, and "not invented here" atmosphere
Listening and diversity, treating people as assets	Selective listening, individual views are status driven, treating people as numbers

Table 9–1 contrasts behaviors that are high in trust-building attributes with behaviors that are low in trust-building attributes. Corporate leaders can use this summary to reflect on current organizational cultures.

Trust is critical to successfully achieving a competent c-commerce culture. Although command- and control-based leadership styles are very much alive today, chief executives need to strive to close the gap from where they are to where they want to be to motivate and retain their talent. Cultures in which trust flourishes have a lower turnover rate than industry norms (12.6% vs. 26%). Without mutual trust and respect among employees and management, c-commerce performance outcomes cannot be achieved.

COMMERCE—FROM TRANSACTIONAL
TO PARTNERING

In successful c-commerce relationships, the individuals, partners, and networks do not treat the relationship as a transaction, but rather as an invested partner. Participants in partnering relationships spend as much time communicating actively, building trust, and promoting mutually successful outcomes as they do working out the intricacies of cost, operational metrics, and performance. They are committed to continuous education about each other's roles and responsibilities. Using c-commerce partnering techniques to create high-performing business processes and long-term success of business relationships depends on the following key factors:

- The skill of the day-to-day management team.
- Quick and effective procedures for raising and resolving issues.
- The quality of the conversations and ability to use metaphors and stories to guide actions, as opposed to competency only in fact-oriented conceptual frames.
- Well-designed c-commerce dimensions that allow for adjustments as business conditions change.

C-commerce is critical to keep individuals, partners, and networks sharing awareness and working together cooperatively through constant change. If relationships deteriorate and conversation and communication is not maintained as a constructive and collaborative business process, capacity to change in the firm will be lost. These problems can be anticipated and avoided. Business processes and relationships must be grounded in a c-commerce model that motivates all parties toward mutual success. Establishing a clear definition of partnering within a c-commerce context is one of the first steps in moving from transactional commerce to partnering commerce.

Collaboration partnerships can take many forms. Whether an informal arrangement or a formal joint venture, such relationships are of great importance. Opportunities can be addressed and significant amounts of new business can be won through cooperative action. The Centre for Competitiveness at the University of Luton (Coulson-Thomas 2004) has examined the approaches of a number of organizations across many sectors and identified critical success factors for managing change. Unsuccessful firms stress the time, effort, and expense required to establish and build relationships, and they often conclude that the likely results do not justify the investment required. Individuals keep to themselves in an attempt to avoid becoming entangled in rivalries and drawn into disputes. Employees of firms that are successful at managing change are more willing to work with colleagues and are more likely to be prepared to cooperate with other complementary suppliers. They see the advantages of collaboration and view collaborating as a means to support learning and development. These firms actively search for potential business partners and explore possibilities for joint initiatives or collective action. They endeavor to find common ground, resolve conflicts, and promote shared interests and goals.

TRANSPARENCY—FROM CONFLICT ORIENTATION TO CONSTRUCTIVE ORIENTATION

Conflict orientation is a common leadership behavior worldwide as the focus on the achievement of tasks and goals dominates time for positive thinking and constructive problem solving. Constructive orientation approaches to developing strong collaborative cultures would include more talking, cooperating, and including stakeholder views. The objective is to create a corporate culture where our reputations and profiles are more transparent, so our behaviors and actions are driven through social networking and trust, improving the reputation of the firm and its leaders. The nature of conflict is often a struggle for control, a desire to overcome an opposing view, a need for domination or power. Conflict always involves opposing forces and different objectives or views. Research supports the effectiveness of multiple conflict management styles and strategies for resolution. Leaders should be skilled in several conflict resolution strategies to have successful results or outcomes. Following are eight steps that will help support constructive conflict resolution using a collaborative leadership style. Assessing the firm's collaborative conflict resolution capabilities will help support future c-commerce growth capabilities.

1. Create a comfortable environment to set the stage for authentic and open dialogue. In expressing conflict, be open by stating views openly, calmly, and as diplomatically as possible. Encourage and invite other stakeholders to do the same. In the beginning, have these conversations face to face versus over the phone. Do not attempt to express conflict in an e-mail because an effective collaborative exchange includes clarification and sharing thoughts and opinions. Too much informal communication is lost in e-mail communication, and e-mails can easily create spirals of ineffective conversations.

2. Define the reasons for conflict partnering together. When defining the problem, use language that works for both parties. Adopting an open, objective, and nondefensive communication approach will help each stakeholder describe the conflict while demonstrating collaborative resolution behaviors. Reflect on specific incidents that better outline the conflict and tell stories using adjectives. The focus of the interaction is learning. Use quality improvement tools such as diagrams to outline the nature of the conflict and identify root causes, or use more informal pictures to visually illustrate the experience in terms that explain the process and emotional context.

3. Communicate personal positions and implications of the situation. Describe feelings as a result of the conflict, and describe the implication this has on trust and desire for realignment. Ensure clear understanding of each stakeholder's position before trying to envision and develop solutions. This step is critical to establishing common ground for problem resolution. Too often people rush to solutions before the problem and personal positions are adequately clarified.

4. Express desire for collaborative reconciliation and resolution. One of the most important foundations to the development of collaborative behaviors is the reinforcement of cooperative intentions. All stakeholders need to be clear about their desire for resolution and commitment to achieving resolution. If everyone shares a desire and commitment to develop mutually agreeable solutions, they will. Reinforcing the importance of the discovery dialogue to improve understanding will be necessary at first.

5. Ensure all stakeholder viewpoints are understood and listened to. Going through the discovery process, if some group is found to be missing, find an appropriate representative and include him or her in the process as soon as possible.

6. Do not rush the process. Taking the time to develop a clear understanding of the conflict and each stakeholder's perspective is important. Rushing conversations will slow down the identification of a shared resolution.

7. Develop solution pathways and identify collaborative and constructive win-win outcomes. As understanding grows, the possibilities of collaborative partnering to resolve conflict can be put into action. The goal is to develop multiple pathways for collaborative resolution and ensure a solution that everyone can support. The final test is adherence to and respect for the chosen resolution.

8. Stop and reflect, and celebrate success. Raise awareness of how the firm is moving along the continuum from conflict orientation to constructive orientation and celebrate those achievements. Celebration generates renewal and acts as a powerful agent for resiliency and risk-taking competency development.

Creating collaborative cultures in which behaviors are more transparent, open, and authentic will require significant investments in leadership development practices. These practices will ensure that collaboration is rooted in all core operating business practices and processes. Migrating from transparent cultures in which conflict orientation is an acceptable operating norm to more constructive and partnering norms requires a fundamental shift in behavior, but the journey is well worth the effort.

NETWORKS—FROM FEW AND LONG TERM TO MANY AND VOLATILE

Efficient relationship network structures have well-understood properties. Historically, people, organizations, communities, and nations have had few networks. Organizations that have very short relationship network paths of information flow and knowledge exchange are able to adapt and change more rapidly. In these organizations, it only takes a few conversations between all the direct and indirect relationships to communicate new information. Long relationship network paths lead to slow processing and distorted information. Understanding the reasons relationships and networks are formed will help address how to strengthen them. Consider the following attributes of effective networks:

- *Similarities.* Relationships will form in the company around common attributes, objectives, or governance.
- *Differences.* Effective relationship networks maintain connections to diverse individuals, teams, functions, and customers. Diversity of relationships is required to maximize innovation in creating stronger collaborative cultures.
- *Multiple communication channels.* A robust relationship network will have several connections between individuals, teams, functions, and customers. If several connections or individual relationships are damaged or removed, other connections exist for uninterrupted information flows between the remaining relationships in the network.
- *Two or three degrees of separation.* The relationship network needs to provide short communication cycles without forcing too many relationships on any one individual, team, function, or customer. This will require that the firm supports both direct and indirect relationships.
- *Prominent relationships.* Some relationships in the network will be more notable or recognizable than others. These relationships have more influence based on the number of direct and indirect connections they facilitate and are critical to expanding and improving the overall relationship network.

Instead of allowing relationship networks to evolve without direction, successful individuals, teams, functions, and customers have found that it pays to actively manage the network. After several years of network building, a stable structure will exist that can link to other well-developed relationship networks in other regions. Mature relationship networks will continue to evolve as people, processes, and knowledge change to match the current work process and c-commerce environment. Attention remains focused on relationship network maintenance and building additional alliances to create new products, services, and markets or to shape and influence policy that will strengthen the work process and c-commerce initiative.

BOUNDARIES—FROM RIGID AND SOLID
TO FLUID AND POROUS

Boundaries are a part of business life. Boundaries exist between functions and cultures, employees and managers, and customers and the firm. Boundaries almost always lead to suboptimal processes, understanding, and solutions. Connected knowledge is an important competitive advantage. The need for fewer global boundaries is accelerating because of a number of current trends; at best, a continued evolution from rigid to more adaptive and fluid business structures is required. Some of these boundary-blurring trends include telecommuting, outsourcing, and economic shifts in research and development.

An article in Australia's *The Age* reported that 44 million U.S. workers will be telecommuting in 2005, either full time or working from home on a part-time basis. The number of telecommuters is expected to grow to 51 million by 2008, with 14 million employees working full time at home. The report noted that the rise in telecommuting has prompted growth in the use of high-speed Internet access by home users. Firms are supporting this movement by subsidizing the equipment and service expenses that allow their employees to work from home.

Boundaries are becoming more fluid because of the increase of outsourcing by firms. Outsourcing is a powerful business strategy for achieving c-commerce business dynamics. As c-commerce business dynamics evolve to become more global, commoditized, instantaneous, and collaborative, outsourcing becomes less a cost-saving strategy and more a c-commerce business model. American companies use outsourcing as an operating strategy to reduce overhead and exposure by shifting spending from internal divisions and capital budgets to external contracts. The outsourcing market is set to grow by 19% through 2005, according to recent market research from Cutting Edge Information. Individual deals involving outsourcing leaders such as IBM have topped $5 billion. Worldwide outsourcing is exceeding $350 billion, with several individual deals exceeding $1 billion. General Electric, General Motors, IBM, Disney, Pfizer and Microsoft save critical resources and spend more time on core competencies through carefully planned, strategically sound outsourcing.

In September 2004, *The Economist* magazine's Economist Intelligence Unit released a report on the globalization of research and development. It asked companies where, outside of their home country, they plan to spend research and development capital. China ranked No. 1, with more than 39% of the firms indicating they will put research and development investment there. From a cultural context, only a few North American firms are carefully thinking through how their cost structure, business models, and competitive positions will fundamentally shift as globalization shifts.

As more c-commerce business strategies are deployed there will be a need for adaptive, and constantly reforming, organizational cultures capable of quickly adapting to change. Knowledge-focused programs such as communities of practice, learning networks, conversation as a competency, and storytelling to increase rapid learning are tools to consider to shift boundaries.

Real-Time Collaboration Enterprise— From Cautious and Methodical to Curious and Adaptive

From a cultural perspective, real-time collaboration enterprises must shift from conservative methodical approaches to problem solving and decision making to collaborative interactions and practices in which change and the ability to adapt are the drivers. C-commerce leverages relationship networks in which communication flows freely through trusted connections. Understanding and maintaining these connections result in improved organizational performance. The effectiveness of relationship networks depends on personal expertise and is enhanced by communication, information flow, and knowledge exchange through direct and indirect relationships. The following are several ways organizations can improve network connectivity and relationships:

- Look for the interrelationships and multiple process functions that individuals possess.
- Know the difference between tacit and explicit knowledge and how it is shared and transferred.

- Reward people for directly sharing their knowledge and including others in the relationship networks.
- Design applications and computer systems that facilitate conversations and sharing of knowledge.
- Help women and minorities connect to information flows, knowledge, and communities in the organization to eliminate difficulties engaging with team members and hindrances to being recognized for accomplishments.
- Recruit new employees through the relationship network of current employees to find individuals that will be able to quickly adjust and establish long-term relationships with the company.
- When transferring employees keep their existing connections in mind to improve diverse network ties and create indirect relationships between teams or functions and greatly improve the flow of information in the company.
- Ensure better coordination of behavior among individuals, teams, functions, and customers by creating indirect relationships to minimize the degree of separation with the relationship network to reduce delays in communication and create alternative communication paths.
- Incorporate new employees into the relationship network right away to ensure that employees and teams connect.

C-commerce ensures competitive advantage. Competitors might duplicate the organizational structure the firm has implemented. However, they will not be able to reproduce the firm's relationship network that drives learning, supports the ability to adjust to changing markets, keeps up with changing customer demands, and continuously improves the effectiveness of the supply chain.

GOVERNANCE—FROM PRESCRIPTIVE TO SELF-REGULATORY

Governance begins as soon as the decision is made to implement new business processes under a c-commerce model. Managing the changes will take commitment from everyone involved. Effective multilevel governance mechanisms to facilitate relationships, service-level management, performance measurements, and supporting tools and business processes are critical to the success of the c-commerce effort. Successful firms share responsibility and accountability for achieving business outcomes and process performance. The work process and c-commerce initiative will work best when the project plan can be executed smoothly, causing minimal disruption to the business and organization.

Implementation of a work process and c-commerce initiative will represent a significant change for employees and the way the firm operates. Managing and leading a firm through this transition can be quite difficult. Forcing through work process and c-commerce initiatives without consulting end users is a critical mistake. In this scenario, end users will see the work process and c-commerce initiative as an enemy trying to impose rules and procedures that they do not understand or want. Users will often openly revolt or act subversively to undermine the work process and c-commerce activities and decisions. If internal behavior needs to change in the firm, exercise strong leadership and change interventions to make it happen. Offer training and other incentives to users who need to see the benefits of change. Executives and senior managers will have to be involved in a hands-on fashion to address user concerns, sort out problems, and keep the peace internally until the benefits of the new way of working become apparent. The bottom line is that work process and c-commerce can be used as tools to support organizational change, but ultimately it is the users of these tools (the employees) who are responsible for making the change happen.

McKinsey Alumni Database—Leveraging Brand and Networks

Leading strategy consultant McKinsey & Company recognized early the value of networks and treating its alumni as part of the company's DNA for life. All McKinsey past employees, "alumni," are encouraged to keep their profile current in the company database. The network is invaluable to McKinsey: for selling to clients, for reaching prior McKinsey employees who are now in senior positions elsewhere, or for helping to find the perfect career match.

Few companies have mastered the power of the alumni network as McKinsey has. Its career matching service posted more than 2300 positions from January to August 2004, a 40% increase from the same period in 2003. At any given time, between 800 and 900 open positions are available, with opportunities for all skill levels. The list includes opportunities from all over the world and continues to expand. The current active board includes opportunities in China, Australia, Central and South America, South Korea, India, Israel, Singapore, Africa, and Eastern Europe.

McKinsey has been leveraging c-commerce approaches to business growth. The company understands the power of its alumni base to enhance its global brand and strengthen its relationship networks. Supporting career development structures is simply another Smart approach to doing business. In talking to McKinsey alumni there is always a sense of pride, identity, and confidence. Many of the alumni we spoke to said things like: "The alumni network helps me keep in touch with colleagues," "I have sourced McKinsey alumni talent living in India to help accelerate our new business model," and "I use the alumni database to support our business development needs." Developing these capabilities to continue to motivate past employees to connect and communicate with one another is an inexpensive investment that further supports collaborative conversations. McKinsey truly understands the power of networks and collaborative ecosystems to increase profitable revenue growth through collaborative commerce transactions.

We highly recommend chief executives invest in alumni databases to continue conversations to support their network intelligence and ensure they keep past employees motivated to recommend their services as they continue to grow in life. People are social creatures, and communities such as the McKinsey Alumni Database tap into people's hearts. Although difficult to quantify, there are many stories of McKinsey partners leveraging the alumni to support their business development client requirements.

EBay—Cultural Values and Community Respect

Founded in 1995, ebay calls itself "the world's online marketplace" for the sale of goods and services. EBay was founded in Pierre Omidyar's San Jose living room in September 1995, conceived from a conversation between Pierre and his wife. An avid Pez collector (she currently boasts a collection of more than 400 dispensers), Omidyar's wife was looking for a place where she could interact with other Pez collectors over the Internet. This was the creative spark that started Omidyar experimenting with the auction format for online person-to-person trading. He created a simple, easy-to-understand mechanism that let buyers and sellers decide the true value of items and connect with others. Today, the eBay community includes more than 135 million registered members worldwide, with transactions totaling more than $100 million a day. On any given day, there are more than 19 million items listed on eBay across 35,000 categories, including fashion, antiques, sports memorabilia, computers, toys, coins, books, magazines, music, pottery, glass, photography, electronics, jewelry, gemstones. From hard-to-find event tickets and cars to picture frames and coffee tables, users can find the unique, the amazing, the collectable, and the practical on eBay.

EBay was founded with the belief that people are honest and trustworthy. The company believes that each of its customers, whether a buyer or a seller, is an individual who deserves to be treated with respect. At a recent conference, eBay CEO Meg Whitman outlined the core values of the eBay culture:

1. We believe that people are basically good.
2. We recognize and respect that everyone is a unique individual.
3. We believe everyone has something to contribute.
4. We encourage people to treat others the way they want to be treated themselves.
5. We believe an open and honest environment can bring the best out of people.

EBay is one of the most successful c-commerce business models. Its core value system is collaborative, and control, hierarchy, and need for power are not included in those core values. EBay is a culture that has developed community-operating principles and has learned the power of the network. The following is a list of some of eBay's community principles:

- Listen to the community.
- Supply follows demand.
- Level playing field.
- People, not wallets.
- Enable, don't direct.
- Many, not few.
- Carrot, not the stick.

EBay is dedicated to its community of members and has numerous services that enhance the trading experience. Ebay's growth comes from meeting and exceeding the expectations of its community members. The company has created a learning culture in which openness and transparency have helped it develop a core culture with tremendous elasticity and agility to collaboratively move with its community stakeholders. Though huge in size, eBay has not lost sight of what originally gave it its competitive advantage: A corporate culture in which collaborative conversations are valued above all else.

View22—Seeing the Big Picture

View22 is a leading provider of collaboration visualization (3D) solutions for Global 2000 firms selling highly configurable, space sensitive products. Leading manufacturers, distributors, and retailers such as GE Healthcare, John Deere, Kohler, Masco, and Pottery Barn use View22's advanced visualization technology to enable their sales forces, contractors, suppliers, and customers to design, plan, configure products, and virtually merchandise their products using an intuitive, easy-to-use Web-based application. View22's technology has helped these companies increase sales by more than 30%. The technology also has helped firms improve organizational productivity by increasing average order values, compressing the sales cycles, and reducing product return rates and installation errors. It also helps design and product management professionals save time and work more collaboratively with their clients.

What is interesting to see with clients using View22 is the change in their interactions with their customers. For example, Kohler customers can log on to the Kohler Web site and visualize the bathroom or kitchen of their choice. They can easily adjust the product selection and color palettes, select additional furnishings to augment the space, send an e-mail to a designer to review and potentially redline recommended improvements, and place the order in real time. In the case of GE, sales representatives used to sell their medical imaging equipment using standard marketing brochures or product catalogs. Clients would identify their needs but could not visualize the end product. CAD/CAM designers would be engaged to get the architectural space layout designs to specification needs, but still the client would not be able to envision in 3D the room layout and equipment positioning, let alone be engaged in an iterative conversation via e-mail.

View22 solutions allow the end consumer to be more closely engaged in the design process and provide increased touch points to extend conversations with sales representatives selling these types of solutions. View22 is an excellent example of a company pioneering new ways of collaborating, merging designers more closely with business practices and bringing immediate value to clients. Conservative payback trends are more than 100% return on investment in less than 9 months. The long-term value of solutions such as View22's is to extend the ecosystem reach of communities to continue the conversations with like-minded consumers, much like eBay has created an infrastructure for ongoing community conversations to guide its future service offerings.

View22 has recently announced that it is integrating its 3D visualization capabilities with WebEx's real-time platform and network. Through this integration, the company will expand its addressable market for 3D collaborative commerce solutions and introduce new applications for the enterprise and consumer markets. As organizations leverage collaborative solutions such as View22, the customer experience changes and shifts radically.

CONCLUSION

In preparing for c-commerce, it is important to analyze the differences between the current culture and the vision of the future culture. It is possible to successfully navigate from the current culture to the c-commerce culture and build relationships along the way. Consider a collection of core existing shared and common values for knowledge sharing, organizational learning, and collaboration within the organization. Encourage diversity in thought and demonstrate the importance of relationships. Collaborate and willingly seek to share knowledge and embrace learning with employees, customers, suppliers, and other stakeholders as often as possible. Understand how work is currently getting done with respect to formal and informal networks. Pay attention to explicit differences in organizational practices such as how work is distributed and how decisions are made. Be certain that differences in culture can be bridged as part of a c-commerce initiative.

Analyze and use relationship and social network approaches to improve communication, learning, innovation, and performance. Encourage competency development in effective dialogue and conversations, leveraging stories and narratives to rapidly guide the organization to new actions. Employees who are collaborative and relationship centric should be sought and recruited for innovation, growth, and learning opportunities. Many c-commerce competencies are not well understood or applied by practicing executives and managers. Assign a knowledgeable executive to be responsible for monitoring the health of the c-commerce cultural ecosystem. He or she should have oversight of relationship network activities, innovation capabilities, knowledge sharing, openness and authenticity, organizational learning, and relationship capital. Developing new cultural competencies and strategic capabilities requires strong leadership.

Chapter 10 introduces measurement correlated to the ten c-commerce capabilities. Performance management is shifting from independent and firm specific to agile and shared across the supply chain. C-commerce considers measurements in several categories for future requirements that will need to be inclusive of partners throughout the value chain. These metrics are extremely valuable as early warning signs of process bottlenecks, performance problems, or changing business conditions that redefine process requirements. C-commerce can be used to provide more complete and sophisticated measures than are currently in use.

10

THE
MEASUREMENT
DIMENSION

The current interest in performance management shows that executives are taking more notice of this factor's importance to success. "What gets measured gets managed" has become a common mantra. Measurement is an important business management tool; it links long-term strategic vision with a set of objectives and then into metrics that influence management action. A well-defined performance or balanced scorecard may sustain a strong working relationship. It is not only a management tool, but also a communication tool. Measurement categories should be applied across the business process and cover both operations and relationships. Be concerned if the only measures being tracked effectively are financial or customer satisfaction metrics. A complete set of performance and improvement metrics includes the following:

- Performance metrics composed of digital capital, process capital, physical capital, information capital, and structural capital.
- Leadership metrics composed of human capital, social capital, customer capital, partner capital, and relationship capital.

	Traditional Approach	C-Commerce Approach
⊃ **Strategy**	Firm First	Customer First
⊃ **Process**	Hierarchical Ownership	Distributed Ownership
⊃ **IT**	Closed and Proprietary	Open and Standards
⊃ **People**	Resource Management	Partnership Management
⊃ **Culture**	Prescriptive	Self-Regulating
⊃ **Measurement**	Firm Shareholder	Value Chain Shareholders

Figure 10–1
Measurement Dimensions

A frequent weakness in balanced scorecard deployments is the lack of rigorous measurement of people, learning, and growth factors.

Several continuing trends confirm that the need for accurate performance management solutions is increasing. There is a widening gap between the market and book value of firms. This gap requires strong leadership. We see continuing growth in the adoption of balanced scorecards and other performance measurement systems for the purposes of nonfinancial measurements and the governance of intangibles, specifically in the reporting of ethics and environmental and sustaining policies.

The development and implementation of measurement systems is a long-term objective. The firm will go through four stages to arrive at an effective set of measurements that are embedded into organizational practice. The first stage is to accept the language and establish a common perspective and internalization of what needs to be measured. The second stage is the adoption of a balanced scorecard model to focus on key performance indicators and agree to spend energy and resources on measurements that can be improved. The third stage is realizing the limitations. All decision makers must make choices without knowing the impact of trade-offs. Many firms are looking at intellectual capital measures to improve the decisions being made. The fourth stage is to link human capital, social capital, relationship capital, leadership capital, partner capital, and customer capital as intellectual capital to shareholder value. This requires that a forecast be created that reflects the linkages

Measurement

	Traditional Approach	C-Commerce Approach
⊃ **Purpose**	Independent	Shared and Agile
⊃ **Identity**	Isolated	Comprehensive
⊃ **Reputation**	Closed	Open
⊃ **Trust**	Contained	Visible
⊃ **Commerce**	Rigid	Adaptive
⊃ **Transparency**	Constrained	Pervasive
⊃ **Networks**	Disconnected	Interconnected
⊃ **Boundaries**	Linear Navigation	Hyperlinked Navigation
⊃ **Real-Time Collaboration**	Static	Dynamic
⊃ **Governance**	Firm Shareholders	Value Chain Shareholders

Figure 10–2
Measurement and Collaboration

and time dependencies of changes in intellectual capital to revenues and cash flows (see Figure 10–2).

The information presented here includes measurements to consider based on the current strategies, goals, and objectives of the firm. A core set of metrics will be shared across the firm and the supply chain. The information presented in this chapter illustrates examples of measurements that can be evaluated as potential core metrics for the firm. The c-commerce capabilities have been mapped to the firm's knowledge innovation and to group measurements for evaluation (see Figure 10–3). The details include the following:

- From independent to shared and agile (purpose) mapped to process capital metrics.
- From isolated to comprehensive (identity) mapped to structural capital metrics.
- From closed to open (reputation) mapped to partner capital metrics.
- From contained to visible (trust) mapped to human capital metrics.
- From rigid to adaptive (commerce) mapped to customer capital metrics.

Knowledge Innovation

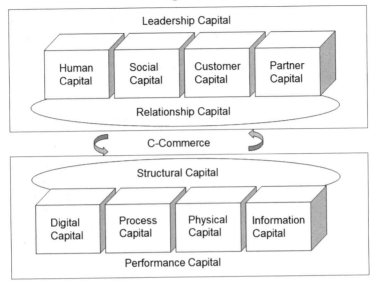

Figure 10–3
Measurements and Potential Core Metrics

- From constrained to pervasive (transparency) mapped to information capital metrics.
- From disconnected to interconnected (networks) mapped to social capital metrics.
- From linear navigation to hyperlinked navigation (boundaries) mapped to digital capital metrics.
- From static to dynamic (real-time collaborative enterprises) mapped to physical capital metrics.
- From firm shareholders to value chain shareholders (governance) mapped to relationship capital metrics.

PURPOSE—FROM INDEPENDENT TO SHARED AND AGILE

Any core business process should have stream of service metrics indicating how the processes are operating. Think across the supply chain. C-commerce metrics need to be inclusive of partners throughout the value chain and be outward looking. We live in a complex, rapidly changing world that requires perspectives and signals from everyone in the value chain or network. The selected metrics are extremely valuable as early warning signs of process bottlenecks, performance problems, or changing business conditions that redefine process requirements. C-commerce may provide the opportunity to upgrade process measurement, sometimes dramatically. If strong process performance capabilities exist with process management maturity, c-commerce can be used to provide more complete and sophisticated measures. Invite customers, partners, and suppliers to discuss metrics and indicators in an open format and develop shared metrics. C-commerce is used across the supply chain to anticipate changes and determine how they will be handled and communicated and how new strategies will be implemented as needed. The types of process capital assessment factors to consider and measurements to define include the following:

- *Integrating value by means of operational excellence.* Business process management plays a critical role in integrating value through operational excellence. This measurement focuses on the effectiveness of work processes, the responsibilities and accountabilities of users performing the work process, and the interaction or transfer from one user to another as the work process is performed. Establish several measurements at critical points within the work process and cycle time across the work process to determine where improvements will be most effective and what the trade-offs might be.
- *Reciprocal points of value.* This is a critical measurement for firms and value chains trying to focus on their core work processes. Often, business units and virtual teams treat all issues and decisions with the same level of urgency. The concern is that all of these issues and decisions are not related to core work processes or competitive advantage for the organization and should be treated differently. If focusing on critical business processes or setting better priorities is a critical concern, consider spending some time evaluating effective reciprocal points of value measurements.

- *Knowledge sharing and knowledge receiving.* Individuals throughout the value chain must have the ability to work on virtual teams and complete assigned activities and tasks through an interactive process of sharing, reciprocity, and openness.
- *Competency mix and alignment with the business model.* An understanding of skills and depth of knowledge is needed to perform the goals and objectives of virtual teams and assigned work process activities and tasks. The objective is to define a baseline of competencies needed to meet key objectives in the business model, measurement of the current mix of skills and competencies available throughout the firm and value chain, and continuous monitoring to improve any identified gaps.
- *Assignment of specialty resources.* If specialty skills and resources exist that are shared across work processes, virtual teams, and the value chain, this could be an important measurement to consider. Once again the goal is resource management and reducing redundant work for these specialty resources.

IDENTITY—FROM ISOLATED TO COMPREHENSIVE

C-commerce requires that firms look at a collection of measurements and share them across the organization and throughout the value chain. As the firm creates a comprehensive view of the organization and begins to respond to new challenges, it will need to be resilient and absorb shifts in strategy, operations, market, and economy. It will be important to be able to measure the composite of the strategy, structure, systems, and processes that enable an organization to respond to environmental changes. The types of structural capital assessment factors to consider and measurements to define include the following:

- *Performance commitment.* The ability to measure and maintain the performance commitment agreed to among the firm and suppliers, customers, partners, and employees can be a critical metric. If there are significant changes over time in the overall performance and quality of knowledge repositories or physical assets, then effects will be evidenced on business goals and objectives.

- *Structural bonds.* This measurement focuses on the ability to measure and maintain the effectiveness of digital and physical assets that are owned within the firm. Digital and physical assets consist of intellectual patents and property, methodologies, and software. Structural bond measurements identify the effectiveness of how well the strategy, structure, systems, and processes are working together.
- *Strategic alignment.* Alignment and a shared vision that coordinates work process objectives with the creation and management of digital assets, the upgrade and support of physical assets, and enterprise information management are critical for the work process and c-commerce initiative to succeed. Establish goals and objectives for business initiatives to coordinate with strategic alignment initiatives and verify that leaders throughout the value chain are converging on this initiative. Consider implementing metrics in this category if there are significant investments or activities around structural capital under way that affect suppliers, partners, or business units.
- *Infrastructure effort invested.* This measurement focuses on the ability to understand the tangible assets that have been invested in employee, supplier, partner, and customer relationships and work processes. This information can be critical to decision-making processes in the firm or value chain; determining the effectiveness of shared applications, systems, and information is crucial.

REPUTATION—FROM CLOSED TO OPEN

Traditionally, the reputation of a firm was based solely on internal factors. The c-commerce firm will need to look at the reputation of the global, collaborative network that links suppliers, contract manufacturers, distributors, partners, and customers. The firm's reputation will no longer be its alone; it will be the collective reputation of the firm and the reputation of the global, integrated virtual enterprise that constitutes the value chain.

C-commerce will expand measurement beyond the firm and throughout the value chain. Of vital importance will be the firm's ability to measure partnership competencies with suppliers, alliances, the community, associations, and other members of the partnership ecosystem. The types of partner capital assessment factors to consider and measurements to define include the following:

- *Interdependence with industries.* The ability to measure the impact of decisions and trade-offs made within the value chain on related industries can be extremely valuable. If decision makers could run simulation models to determine the effects of their choices, then wiser choices and better decisions would result. In industries that are very volatile and change quickly this measure should be established in the short term.

- *Communication among suppliers, distributors, and business partners.* This measurement concerns the abstracting or summarizing of communication that has occurred throughout the value chain on specific topics relevant to an individual's multiple personas. These abstracts can trigger additional conversations or alter decisions and activities as part of completing activities and tasks. The objective is to measure the adoption and use of these abstracts and measure how the use of this information affected actions or decisions.

- *Formal versus informal agreement status.* The measurement of formal versus informal agreements benefits continuity. Too many exceptions have to be addressed in services levels and work processes when agreements throughout the firm and value chain vary significantly. Determine if this is a critical partnership capital metric to implement.

- *Diversification index.* Deciding when to diversify is never easy. For a strong revenue stream, the firm and the value chain need to be focused on growth, customer satisfaction, and shareholder value. Establish the need for metrics associated with development, diversification, and growth to be or remain competitive in the marketplace.

- *Collaboration versus cooperation-competition classification.* Challenges with competition among business units within the organization and among firms within the value chain are included here. It is important that competition expands beyond the firm and the supply chain and into the industry. Determine if measurements in this category will be of significant value and establish metrics moving forward as needed.

Trust—From Contained to Visible

Trust is a composite measurement of the knowledge, skills, and experiences of the firm's employees and contractors. In most firms this knowledge is contained in functional business areas. By using c-commerce, the human capital throughout the value chain can be brought together as an engine of innovation. The firm's ability to apply its human capital to solve business problems allows knowledge to be put into action. The types of human capital assessment factors to consider and measurements to define include the following:

- *Skills, knowledge, intellect, and creativity.* The firm's leaders need an awareness and some level of assurance that the firm has people with the appropriate skills, knowledge, intellect, and creativity to successfully achieve targeted goals and objectives. The measurement objective is to understand how skills and knowledge change over time and continuously monitor and improve learning and recruiting practices.
- *Personality profile mix.* This measurement is about diversity and creating appropriate action plans when conflicts between people arise. The goal is to recognize the value of differences and how they affect decision making and how work gets done. We have all worked with individuals who are difficult to interact with. These problems have to be dealt with quickly and effectively. It is not possible to eliminate conflict; rather, the desired result is to identify the conflicts so that they can be resolved.
- *Employee loyalty index.* Most firms work very hard to be a good employer and want their employees to enjoy working for the organization. Many firms conduct employee surveys to understand the key issues employees are dealing with. They also monitor employee retention statistics and goals. The firm will create action plans that include desired results for improvement. The measurement objective is to monitor the execution of the action plans and evaluate how effective the results are in improving the targeted employee issues.
- *Total rewards and accountability programs.* Reward and recognition programs are a good way to measure human

capital and trust. External benchmarks are frequently needed for reward and accountability programs to determine if the benefit the firm is offering is competitive in the industry.

- *Workplace productivity.* The performance and productivity measurement is extremely effective if cost is the primary business driver. Measure the performance of targeted work processes, implement continuous improvement and change management plans, and monitor the results for the desired improvements.

- *Recruiting and retention excellence.* Measuring the effectiveness of recruiting and retention processes can be very helpful. Measurements that track how quickly positions are filled can be relatively easy to identify. It is much more challenging to measure the effectiveness of skill utilization for employees and contractors. Use cause and effect analysis to determine where measurements can be applied to provide insight and assistance for improvement.

COMMERCE—FROM RIGID TO ADAPTIVE

Commerce is driven by customer capital. It is the knowledge of channels, customer preferences, trends, and competitive intelligence. There are aspects of brand capital incorporated into understanding customers. Customer satisfaction is measured in terms of demands customers make on the firm for products and services. These demands are managed in the organization through available human and structural capital processes that might appear as a change in distribution channels and service levels. Development and growth are often realized by an increase in intellectual capital. Tapping into the customer base helps discover new preferences, changes, and applications. Customer and consumer capital is about loyalty: loyalty to the brand and to the customer's customer. The types of customer capital assessment factors to consider and measurements to define include the following:

- *Loyalty measures.* This is the ability to measure the loyalty of customers. It is important that customers are segmented. Some customers are most favored and valued, and other customers are not as valued. Customers that require special products or services or require the execution of exception processes to meet their demands might be more expensive to keep than to turn away. The measurement of customer service is critical. Customers are most loyal to firms that have effectively resolved issues when they occurred. Define loyalty measures, segment customers, and improve shareholder value as defined action plans and marketing campaigns are executed.

- *Continuity over time.* The implementation of service management and the ability to manage the associated service levels are covered in this measurement category. Service levels need to be coordinated with suppliers, partners, and customers throughout the value chain to maximize effectiveness across the supply chain.

- *Relationship quality index.* For favored and valued customers the quality of those relationships needs to be measured and deepened over time. Establish relationship owners and monitor the effectiveness of these key relationships over time.

- *Certainty and confidence indicators.* This is the ability to measure the intended customer experience and the perceived product and service quality by the customer. The perception of the customer is critical for verbal endorsements and references of products and services to others. Establish the intended certainty and confidence indicators for selected product and services, establish any required action plans to improve customer confidence, and continue to monitor and measure consumer confidence.

Transparency—From Constrained to Pervasive

The goal of transparency is to leverage information available throughout the firm, supply chain, and Internet into search results, work processes, and collaborative exchanges. Enterprise content management, knowledge management, business intelligence, and other information intensive activities are making digital assets more available. The types of information capital assessment factors to consider and measurements to define include the following:

- *Intellectual property management.* This measure addresses the lifecycle of intellectual assets. Intellectual patents and property, methodologies, policies, and other content that is considered critical to the firm are included in this measurement. If there is significant security, localization of intellectual property sharing, workflow to approve, or assets to catalog, then measurements in this area should be considered. Establish intellectual property management measurements where significant challenges exist or where regulatory requirements need to be met.
- *Complementary information sharing.* It is often the case that when one resource is working through a defined activity or task another virtual team or work process would benefit from some or all of the work being completed. This is an important measurement if the primary business driver is cost. Determine if resolving this issue is critical to the success of the firm or value chain, and implement this metric if needed.
- *Technology flows.* It is important to be able to measure the integration of applications, systems, and information throughout the supply chain. Consider this measurement if there is a significant number of human–system interactions. Evaluate and select manual activities that can be automated. Establish technology flow measurements where significant challenges exist; these measures provide an excellent opportunity for continuous improvement.
- *Knowledge flows.* Once technology measurements are established and functioning within an acceptable range, it is important to measure the interaction of people within applications, systems, and information. This function is designed to measure, maintain, and improve the availability and reuse of information available within the value chain.

NETWORKS—FROM DISCONNECTED TO INTERCONNECTED

In firms today there are pervasive communities of practice and informal relationship networks. Significant benefits are to be realized by developing c-commerce and formal relationship networks within the value chain. C-commerce introduces social capital as the newest form of measurement in understanding how to develop and manage relationship capital. To focus on these interconnected network opportunities, social capital measurements need to be established. The types of social capital assessment factors to consider and measurements to define include the following:

- *Transferring resources among virtual teams.* In the c-commerce organization, effective virtual teams are critical to success. Resources must be managed across the value chain to improve the flexibility and effectiveness of virtual teams. Determine if resource management across the value chain is critical to meeting desired goals and objectives and implement this metric when needed.

- *Community of practice capabilities and identity profiling.* The analysis of resource allocation is always challenging, but it is worth the effort because it is used to determine skills and knowledge of employees, community of practice participation, knowledge transfer, and other activities and tasks. When resource allocation is a critical success factor, evaluate how identity management will be used to facilitate the solution. Identity profiling will be an enterprise solution and service that will need to be monitored and managed. Establish a measurement, set goals and objectives, and continue to improve over time.

- *Collaborative closeness within communities.* Communities of practice play a critical role as the building blocks for creating, sharing, and applying organizational knowledge. Once communities of practice become recognized by the firm, both knowledge and human capital can be leveraged. These communities are also instrumental in establishing the web of social relationships needed to influence individual behavior to stimulate economic growth. If a critical measurement is needed to develop strong structural, relational, and cognitive dimensions in relationship networks within the firm or value chain, then this is a metric to consider. This measurement closes the gaps in the creating, sharing, and applying of knowledge.

- *Social bonds.* These metrics are associated with informal relationships and the number of relationships required for finding or sharing information throughout the firm or value chain.

■ *Commitment indicator.* The transformation from a traditional firm to a c-commerce firm will require a significant number of change management activities and milestones. It is important that managers create a level of commitment for this effort and continue to nurture enthusiasm for the activities. Establish some measurements around the change management plan and ensure that the desired level of commitment to the business model is maintained.

BOUNDARIES—FROM LINEAR NAVIGATION TO HYPERLINKED NAVIGATION

Establishing links to relevant information throughout the value chain is critical to meeting the goals and objectives of the work process and c-commerce initiative. The strategic framework of digital capital is the codified knowledge available in the firm. Digital capital establishes the boundaries of a hyperlinked navigation solution. The emphasis is on looking at knowledge management infrastructure tools to support and improve the flow and sourcing of knowledge. The types of digital capital assessment factors to consider and measurements to define include the following:

■ *Interaction between technology and organizational forms.* Human capital is frequently the most expensive resource. When people are being used to extract, transfer, move, and load information from one system into another, there is an opportunity for improvement. Potential areas of improvement include error reduction, process performance improvements, cost reduction for human capital resources, and using people as information intermediaries when the information speaks for itself.
■ *Contingency and recovery.* The current focus on legal and regulatory requirements associated with digital assets is causing significant advancements to be made in the area of contingency and recovery. This measurement demonstrates progress to meet compliance objectives.
■ *Intuitive usage aligns with expectations.* Codified knowledge needs to be stored, cataloged, and indexed. The rules and policies associated with how information is created,

where it is stored, and when it is archived or destroyed can be complicated. Where possible, these rules and policies should be automated for users.

■ *Open standards.* The ability to extract, transform, move, and load information from one system to another is a critical integration requirement. Open standards are used to provide consistent content between applications, systems, gateways, and other interfaces. Consider implementing data migration and quality measurements to monitor the increased use of open standards and reduced complexity of the information technology landscape.

REAL-TIME COLLABORATION ENTERPRISE— FROM STATIC TO DYNAMIC

The c-commerce virtual organization requires a worldwide data-sharing network. It will be more than a transactional exchange. The desired result is a transparent view of interenterprise supply chain planning and inventory systems. Using enabling technologies, different systems will have to be connected to enable real-time information flow. By aggregating and analyzing shared applications and systems, firms throughout the value chain can provide early advisories on supply chain issues that include details of the overall impact, linkage to customer orders, on-demand report generation, and suggested intelligent resolution options.

Consider solutions that provide supply chain partners with alerts and escalation mechanisms so that potential problems can be resolved before they disrupt the value chain. A common place to start is with data and information sharing around supply chain management and workflow and analysis applications. Once successful goals and objectives are achieved, consider capabilities of design collaboration, component lifecycle management, and demand chain integration. The types of physical capital assessment factors to consider and measurements to define include the following:

■ *Operational flexibility and adaptability.* The integration of applications and systems across the information technology infrastructure increases operational flexibility and adaptability. It can also increase the difficulty of maintaining and upgrading hardware and software because of the interconnectivity of software versions, applications running on servers, and interactions and dependencies applications have on each other. Several support and maintenance measurements will need to be established to manage the information technology environment.

- *Real-time fulfillment enablement.* System and application integration is happening across the supply chain. Orders are automatically created in one firm and then automatically filled in the warehouse of another firm without any human intervention. Open standards, shared applications, and information exchanges are making this possible, and measurements need to be established and shared across the supply chain to make certain these solutions are performing as expected.

- *Coordinated dispersed geographical facilities.* Applications are hosted by external vendors, and entire information technology departments are outsourced and managed in another country. Coordinating work processes and decisions across the globe can be significant depending on globalization and sourcing of products and services by the firm. If work processes are shared across multiple countries or partners throughout the supply chain, several shared metrics should be considered.

- *Resilience to demand levels.* Storing, cataloging, indexing, and retrieving digital assets can use a significant number of information technology resources. Keeping up with the increasing number of digital assets that are created across the firm requires planning. Consider measurements in this category to monitor enterprise content management goals and objectives.

GOVERNANCE—FROM FIRM SHAREHOLDERS TO VALUE CHAIN SHAREHOLDERS

The c-commerce governance model is the measurement of relationship capital. The intellectual capital contained within relationship capital is critical. Without aligned leadership and vision, human behaviors cannot be aligned to the vision of the firm or the value chain. With alignment it is possible to manage intangible assets and the behavior that best fosters the creation of knowledge and innovation throughout the value chain. The types of relationship capital assessment factors to consider and measurements to define include the following:

- *Leadership style consistency and sustainability.* There is nothing more confusing to employees and managers throughout the firm than conflicting objectives, messages, and priorities from leaders. These conflicting messages do not necessarily mean that leaders are misaligned; often the problem lies in ineffective communication delivered through the organization. If leadership styles appear inconsistent in the firm or once-aligned leaders seem to diverge, metrics in this category would be worth evaluating.
- *Network management ecosystems.* These are measurements to determine the linkages and effectiveness of relationships through the firm, value chain, and industry. An effective c-commerce initiative will eventually want to actively manage relationship networks from the supplier's supplier to the customer's customer.
- *Congruence of values.* People throughout the firm and value chain have individual values and drivers. This is an example of how differences will be valuable in the long term. In the short term it is useful to document and internalize overall corporate values to provide a framework of how work gets done throughout the supply chain. The metrics associated with congruence of values will determine the degree to which the values have been instilled in the behavior and decision making of employees.
- *Balance of creative tension.* These measurements encapsulate the ability to identify the stress or tension associated with change in the firm and across the value chain. There has to be a healthy balance within the firm or value chain to maximize performance.
- *Governance practices.* Distributed decision-making models will be established across the value chain and governance models will be established to facilitate execution and enable virtual teams. Define measures to determine the effectiveness of governance practices once they are established.

Selecting Critical Measures

Traditional accounting measures do not meet the complete measurement needs of the firm. They measure only tangible assets, not intangible assets. With respect to action focus they are almost never used as a management tool. Firms view the annual statement as historical reporting for compliance purposes, and internal management accounting is dealt with separately. C-commerce requires firms to look at a collection of measurements to focus and improve the use of business processes that are supported by digital assets, information management, and physical assets.

These scorecard metrics should provide snapshots that are used to identify trends and recognize fluctuations based on differences in business cycles. The results should trigger the creation of action plans to resolve performance issues. There are times when external factors or significant changes in individual variables will have to be calculated into performance, business, and relationship results. Consider dimensions of structural capital to get a complete picture of work process effectiveness through service level agreement performance. A balanced scorecard for tracking the performance and health of structural capital should include the following:

- *Specific contract terms.* The objective is to measure how effective the work process is meeting performance objectives and customer service level agreements. Based on the agreed-on products and services that the firm is expected to deliver, the performance-based measurements should include cost, cycle times, response times, and any other terms that are specifically outlined in the contract.
- *Business outcomes.* The measurement is to define how well the relationships that deliver products, services, and customer intimacy are returning value in terms of cost, focus, or flexibility. For example, if the primary business driver is focus, then measurements will need to establish how well focus has improved. Is the company spending more time on mission-critical customer-focused core processes? These metrics can be either quantitative or qualitative as long as they measure the effectiveness and efficiency of work on the primary driver.

- *Relationship quality.* These measurements are focused on how well individuals, teams, functions, and partners are meeting their commitments to making relationships work. These metrics are based on relationship types of employees, partnerships, or alliances to determine the health and productivity of working relationships. How well is everyone living up to the responsibilities to participate, communicate, and resolve problems expeditiously?

To summarize, developing c-commerce measurement strategies requires a balance of metric types. Leveraging balanced scorecard approaches is helpful, but we also encourage applying other measurement techniques including social networking analytics for measuring network health and narrative storytelling techniques to ensure both tacit and explicit forms of knowledge flow are captured.

Supply Chain Collaboration and Demand Forecasting

One critical success factor in supporting operational planning assumptions is building real-time linkages for early access to sales data that ensures more accurate and frequent demand forecasts from major customers. This is a challenging process. Organizations continue to have difficulty in forecasting sales data against original forecasts, and often major gaps exist in the outlook forecasting data versus the actual results.

The most important supply chain metrics based on our research are the following:

- Demand forecast accuracy.
- Perfect order fulfillment. (Perfect means complete, accurate, and on time.)
- Supply chain cost.
- Cash-to-cash cycle time.

These critical metrics are used by the company to get a quick, balanced snapshot of its supply chain performance. These metrics allow the firm to determine demand and effectiveness of the trade-offs between cost and service combined with cash flow management. Demand forecast accuracy creates high responsiveness and cuts costs right through the supply chain. Companies that are best at demand forecasting average 15% less inventory, 17% stronger perfect order fulfillment, and 35% shorter cash-to-cash cycle times, while having a tenth of the stock-outs of their peers. Demand forecast accuracy correlates with perfect order fulfillment: A 1 percentage point improvement in demand forecast accuracy can yield a 2 percentage point improvement in perfect order fulfillment capability. Even a minor improvement in a company's demand visibility can have a dramatic effect on its customer responsiveness.

Fortunately, some companies are getting the real-time linkages for demand forecasting accuracy right. For example, Colgate-Palmolive has linked its enterprise resource planning system to cash registers in Wal-Mart. Through these links Colgate-Palmolive monitors sales in close to real time and keeps its production plans current. As a result, the company's demand forecasts are 98% accurate and it has saved $150 million a year by reducing its inventory by 13%.

Pirelli Tyres, which operates in 120 countries and has annual revenues of $3 billion, has provided its distributors with access to its supply chain management, production planning, and finance applications. Large distributors get application-to-application links via middleware from Tibco Software, and small ones get a customized Web site. These links provide the following:

- *Faster sales forecasting.* It used to take 70 days to obtain sales forecasts from all the distributors and create a new production plan; now it takes just 30 minutes.
- *Smaller tire stocks at distributors (which Pirelli finances).* Stocks have been reduced by 20%. Automated reordering reduces the time needed for delivering replacement stock.
- *Faster creation of key performance indicators.* This used to take 90 days but now takes 30 minutes, improving decision making.

CONCLUSION

Performance management has shifted organizations from a command-and-control to a facilitation model of leadership. The scope of business analytics begins with a clear insight on who the users are, what metrics are associated with the processes that they manage, and what logic or rules apply when analyzing the status and effectiveness of these processes. When determining partnerships and user segmentation it is important to understand the various roles and levels of experience that the participants bring to analyzing associated business data and processes. The factors will outline the design needed to accommodate these users through online resources tailored to their roles. Supply chain processes, user segmentation, profiling, and analysis are used to establish the key performance indicators that will be both adoptable by the user constituents and valuable to the value chain in terms of impact. The result is business intelligence around what partners need to know, using available data assets in a collaborative decision-making business model that leverages available resources.

In Part III we look at the ten c-commerce capabilities and provide practical suggestions to improve a firm's current position. In addition, we present a c-commerce quick assessment guide that can be used to assess where a firm is in its c-commerce journey. The c-commerce assessment guide offers practical suggestions to evaluate the firm's current state and work toward gap closure. The objective is to use the material in the book to create a c-commerce vision, combined with the c-commerce starting point, to create a list and roadmap that can be used to design the work process and c-commerce initiative for the firm. Chapter 11 takes a look at each c-commerce capability. Suggestions are provided on how to make c-commerce improvements in purpose, identity, reputation, trust, commerce, transparency, networks, boundaries, real-time collaboration enterprise, and governance.

PART III

THE IMPLEMENTATION PATH

11

C-COMMERCE: GETTING STARTED

This chapter focuses on how to ensure the establishment of a sound foundation for c-commerce in the organization. It is structured around the ten categories of c-commerce capabilities introduced in Chapter 3. For each area, we provide suggestions for policies and processes that will ease the firm's transition to c-commerce.

The c-commerce quick assessment introduced at the end of the chapter is a valuable tool for analyzing how a firm can best use c-commerce for competitive advantage. It can lead to significant changes such as the implementation of a knowledge management and collaboration program within a work process initiative. Use the assessment results to improve existing communication, change management, and institute continuous improvement plans by incorporating c-commerce capabilities into these activities.

Whatever the goals and objectives of your organization, there are ways that c-commerce can provide value. With each of the ten c-commerce capabilities, there is a scale to assess the areas in which a firm is effectively incorporating c-commerce and the areas in which it could focus on to implement c-commerce improvements. Rank the firm on the scale for each of the six key dimensions, and calculate the average for that capability. Depending on the particular needs of your firm (determined with the help of the assessment tool), choose from among the recommended solutions to maximize your c-commerce advantage.

CATEGORY 1: PURPOSE

Successful collaboration, business dynamics, and networks are all built from a shared purpose. If the purpose is well understood and agreed on by individuals, firms, and partners throughout the value chain, then shared objectives can be established in which interactions function effectively and desired results can be achieved. The following will help strengthen the firm's c-commerce purpose:

- Expand the organization's strategy to clearly include and communicate a purpose that supports the social and information technology (IT) networks' goals and objectives. Purpose supplies an organizational theme. For example, Walt Disney's purpose is to bring happiness to millions. Add components to the diversity program and communication plan to understand the different ways purpose is

Purpose

	1	2	3	4	5	6	7
⊃ **Strategy**	Company versus Company					Network versus Network	
⊃ **Process**	Products and Services					Relationship Centric Processes	
⊃ **IT Infrastructure**	Firm Centric					Value Chain Centric	
⊃ **People**	Task						Goals
⊃ **Culture/Change**	Uniformity						Diversity
⊃ **Measurement**	Independent					Shared and Agile	

Figure 11–1
Purpose and Collaboration

being implemented within the firm or across the supply chain.

- Make certain that people understand how the tasks they perform map to the firm's purpose. Broaden the definition and understanding of business processes to include information about the relationship network used to support them. Expand awareness of how a shared purpose is providing value both internally and externally. Make certain the IT infrastructure can support the exchange of information among suppliers, partners, and others associated with the supply chain to strengthen purpose-driven achievement.

CATEGORY 2: IDENTITY

People identify themselves in many different ways. Who they are, what they need, what they do, and what they like are questions related to aspects of leadership, parenting techniques and family dynamics, job responsibilities and performance, competencies and certifications, community involvement, and vacation and entertainment activities. The complexity and effectiveness of personal profiles will continue to drive and affect future marketing programs. The firm's c-commerce identity will benefit from the following:

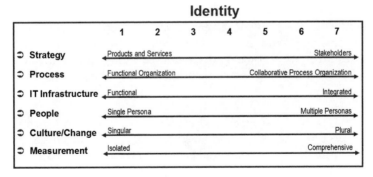

Figure 11–2
Identity and Collaboration

- Focus on knowledge-management activities and best practices. Develop a better sense of the people in the firm and across the supply chain to understand identity. Establish subject-expert profiling techniques to more easily source the know-how in the organization. Support the development and evolution of communities of practice to understand how work gets done and what priorities are. Use document management solutions, best practice sharing, idea capturing, instant messaging, teleconferencing, and other collaborative tools and techniques to raise identity awareness.

- Create an identity management program. Take advantage of user profiles to understand how existing applications and systems can be used more broadly in the firm or across the supply chain. Create a single sign-on environment for users so they will not have to open and log on to many applications and systems to do their jobs. Use these personal profiles with the intranet and portal pages to present only the activities and tasks needed by the user. For example, each user interacts only with the specific processes in PeopleSoft or SAP that are relevant to performing their jobs or areas of responsibility.

CATEGORY 3: REPUTATION

Reputation is about character. An organization's or industry's reputation is related to how its stakeholders—customers, investors, employees, and the media—view such factors as product quality, management, financial performance, social responsibility, and market leadership. A reputation is built and earned over time and cannot be easily acquired. Consider the following when focusing on the firm's c-commerce reputation:

- Update the strategy and communication plans to include specific activities and tasks to successfully manage the complexity of a c-commerce organization. Reputation is complex and consists of an interdependency of assets, core competencies, image, and strategic alliances that cannot be easily separated from each other. Develop an integrated

Reputation

	1	2	3	4	5	6	7
⊃ Strategy	Easy to Manage					Complex to Manage	
⊃ Process	Product Experience					Customer Relationships	
⊃ IT Infrastructure	Reliable and Specific					Agile and Flexible	
⊃ People	Individual					Network	
⊃ Culture/Change	Narrow					Comprehensive	
⊃ Measurement	Closed					Open	

Figure 11–3
Reputation and Collaboration

package of collaborative policies and solutions for leaders, partners, and relationship networks.

- Establish a rapid application development environment within the IT infrastructure to quickly respond to and implement change. Distribute intranet and extranet publishing across the firm. Establish automated reviews of content to make certain that appropriate content lifecycle and security policies and procedures are enforced. Make certain that the appropriate governance model is available to provide the checks and balances that are needed.

CATEGORY 4: TRUST

Trust is the core value that establishes the balance among strategy, people, process, and systems. Trust is the ultimate motivator and is gained through experience. When expectations are well defined and individuals deliver what they have communicated or promised, trust increases. People are motivated to cooperate with individuals that they trust. To enhance trust within your c-commerce framework consider the following recommendations:

- Monitor employee attitudes and work to reduce conflict and confusion; improve communications to increase reciprocity. Create action plans to address issues that

Trust

	1	2	3	4	5	6	7
⊃ **Strategy**	Underestimated Value						Core Value
⊃ **Process**	Image and Employee Loyalty				Brand, Emotion, and Reciprocity		
⊃ **IT Infrastructure**	Narrow Picture						Holistic Picture
⊃ **People**	Power						Knowledge
⊃ **Culture/Change**	Selective						Inclusive
⊃ **Measurement**	Contained						Visible

Figure 11–4
Trust and Collaboration

employees identify as needing improvement. Empower focus groups, diversity programs, communities of practice, and other teams to define and implement the most appropriate action plans.

- Make certain the firm's remuneration and recognition program rewards sharing information and knowledge. If knowledge is power and c-commerce empowers the individual, firm, or supply chain, then finding effective ways to store, find, and manage information is critical. Consider using compliance programs such as Sarbanes-Oxley and enterprise content management to improve access to and sharing of information.

CATEGORY 5: COMMERCE

Commerce in collaboration is about sharing and exchanging information to create knowledge. Focusing on the primary delivery methods will produce the most effective results. The three major knowledge flow and exchange levers are reciprocity, dynamic real-time exchange, and conversation quality. The following strategies will help enhance the commerce in c-commerce:

Commerce

	1	2	3	4	5	6	7
⊃ **Strategy**	Win-Lose						Win-Win
⊃ **Process**	Product Lifecycle Driven				Customer and Supply Chain Driven		
⊃ **IT Infrastructure**	Proprietary						Standards
⊃ **People**	Transactional and Operational					Growth and Learning	
⊃ **Culture/Change**	Transactional						Partnering
⊃ **Measurement**	Rigid						Adaptive

Figure 11–5
Commerce and Collaboration

- Assess how information is exchanged in teams and throughout the inter- and intraorganizational business processes. Review existing knowledge management and collaboration action plans being executed across the firm to make sure they are consistent and not mutually exclusive or in conflict with each other. Encourage consistent ways to improve reciprocity, dynamic real-time exchanges, and conversation quality within business processes shared across the firm and the supply chain.
- Make certain that business processes are driven by customer relationships and supply chain goals and objectives. Review the focus of business processes. In many cases, they will be entirely focused on the deliverables created and measured financially. To consider c-commerce improvement in business processes, focus on the customer relationship value. If the current deliverable and cost lens does not easily reflect the value of customer relationships and supply chain goals and objectives, then change the lens of the business process.

Category 6: Transparency

Transparency is about communicating clearly. For c-commerce to succeed, it is vital that everyone who needs information is informed and can easily access the details they need. Because

Transparency

	1	2	3	4	5	6	7
⟳ **Strategy**	Competitive Intelligence & Protection			Shared Intelligence & Risk Management			
⟳ **Process**	Closed and Dispersed					Open and Adaptive	
⟳ **IT Infrastructure**	Application Centric					Personalized Delivery	
⟳ **People**	Six Degrees of Separation				Two Degrees of Separation		
⟳ **Culture/Change**	Conflict Orientation					Constructive Orientation	
⟳ **Measurement**	Constrained					Pervasive	

Figure 11–6

Transparency and Collaboration

stakeholders have a vested interest in the business process or strategic plan, each of them needs to be kept informed of developments relevant to them. When focusing on the firm's c-commerce transparency consider the following:

- Add a work process and c-commerce initiative into an existing program. Assess the benefits of adopting new business dynamics using collaboration, people, and relationship networks. If developing stronger partnerships in the industry to quickly adjust to changes in the marketplace is important, then begin planning for the future. Think big and start small by improving relationship networks, reciprocity, trust, or other c-commerce advantages in existing work processes or virtual team activities.
- Design and deploy an enterprise portal that can be personalized to meet the needs of employees, customers, partners, and others. Expanding the information and knowledge available to individuals, business units, virtual teams, partners, and customers will increase confusion or add complexity within the organization if knowledge flow is not streamlined to personal needs. To mitigate this risk, implement well-designed enterprise portal pages with several configuration options to allow personalization by the individual user. Communications, collaboration, and other changes can be delivered through the enterprise portal and help manage expectations.

CATEGORY 7: NETWORKS

Today we live in a world of networks. From networks of suppliers to networks of computers and from networks of trading partners to networks of activists, the world is hyperlinked and many are taking advantage of these connections. The social nexus provides individuals, customers, and firms with information insight and opportunities. The firm's c-commerce networks will benefit from the following actions:

- Focus on relationship network activities and best practices using virtual teams to complete projects. Create a map of the social network in the organization, leveraging best practices in social network analysis and design. Determine which relationships are critical to maintain and which new relationships need to be established. Make certain that communications can be effectively shared across the organization in two or three degrees of separation using the relationship network. Create specific deliverables and types of interactions needed to build strong, global virtual teams.
- Leverage social networking analytic approaches to evaluate the health of networks. To promote diversity and gain the broad perspective needed to implement an adaptive c-commerce organization, take advantage of social networking software solutions and analysis techniques to

Networks

	1	2	3	4	5	6	7
⊃ Strategy	Source of Cost					Source of Growth	
⊃ Process	Power Centric					Knowledge Centric	
⊃ IT Infrastructure	Limited Access Bandwidth			Multilayered Access and Broadband			
⊃ People	Business Units and Functional Teams			Business Processes and Virtual Teams			
⊃ Culture/Change	Few and Long-Term					Many and Volatile	
⊃ Measurement	Disconnected					Interconnected	

Figure 11–7
Networks and Collaboration

understand and improve the social nexus. Design working teams to include team members and stakeholders from multiple business units or firms throughout the supply chain to increase collaborative experiences and promote diversity. Make certain that shared metrics and collaboration solutions are available for virtual teams across the globe so they can learn from each other, measure their effectiveness, and work together.

CATEGORY 8: BOUNDARIES

Boundaries establish the guidelines we work within; they are always shifting. The key to boundaries is to focus on the present, using a clear set of rules and guidelines to achieve the growth and success needed now, yet allow the flexibility to plan effectively for the future. This will help to ensure that the rules and guidelines can easily expand or change over time as the firm evolves. When focusing on the firm's c-commerce boundaries consider the following:

- Design and implement an open business intelligence program that tracks c-commerce key performance indicators. Establish report notification, enterprise reports, management reports, operational reports, and decision support to manage risk within the organization. Use business

Boundaries

	1	2	3	4	5	6	7
⊃ Strategy	Local						Global
⊃ Process	Clear						Opaque
⊃ IT Infrastructure	Ivory Tower and Data Centric				Collaborative and Process Centric		
⊃ People	Formal and Physical				Formal, Informal, and Virtual		
⊃ Culture/Change	Rigid and Solid				Fluid and Porous		
⊃ Measurement	Linear Navigation				Hyperlinked Navigation		

Figure 11–8
Boundaries and Collaboration

analysts, trends, simulations, and other tools available to use the past to predict and plan for the future. Ensure that the right boundaries, rules, and guidelines are in place for individuals, teams, business units, and partners to be effective.

- Change executive leadership C-level roles (chief executive officer, chief operating officer, chief marketing officer) that demonstrate desired behavior. Lead by example. Make certain that senior managers and executives understand c-commerce goals and objectives. They should use virtual meeting solutions, e-mail, enterprise content management applications, and other relationship network techniques that employees throughout the organization are expected to use. This alone will go a long way to making sure those c-commerce goals and objectives become ingrained in how work gets done into the future.

CATEGORY 9: REAL-TIME COLLABORATION ENTERPRISE

Real-time collaboration enterprises are virtual organizations with the ability to quickly align business partners and assets. They are able to deliver products or services through internal, direct, or outsourced models, and they exploit competitive

Real-Time Collaboration Enterprise

	1	2	3	4	5	6	7
Strategy	Slow and Cyclical					Fast and Iterative	
Process	Sequential					Dynamic and Iterative	
IT Infrastructure	One-to-One, -Many, Asynchronous			Plus Many-to-Many, Plus Synchronous			
People	Single Dimensional					Multidimensional	
Culture/Change	Cautious and Methodical					Curious and Adaptive	
Measurement	Static					Dynamic	

Figure 11–9
Real-Time Enterprise and Collaboration

advantage when new opportunities emerge. The following will help support the firm's c-commerce real-time collaboration enterprises:

- Establish a business process management program. Include business process reengineering, customer relationship management, and supply chain management requirements to migrate from a products and services perspective to a stakeholder perspective. Take advantage of the relationships identified to communicate and share information more effectively. Include information about how changes in work processes affect various people, both upstream and downstream, in the work flow.
- Increase integration of the IT infrastructure. There are a couple of choices available to reduce complexity in the IT environment. The process is to define enterprise applications and systems, move users onto the enterprise systems, and archive or turn off departmental solutions. Enterprise applications and systems will be combined to meet the business needs of the firm. Enterprise and supply chain applications and systems will require integration. Rather than having users manually enter information from one system to another, extraction, transformation, move, and load programs need to be created and maintained.

Category 10: Governance

The c-commerce governance model will need to manage people and collaboration, business dynamics, and the building and leveraging of collaborative networks. To help with these c-commerce governance tasks, consider these suggestions:

- Appoint an executive accountable for collaborative business strategies. All corporate initiatives require an executive sponsor with the appropriate access to funding and resources. The c-commerce initiative is no different. Find an executive who understands the value of adapting quickly to changes in the marketplace by using new business models that are supported by leveraging networks of people.

Governance

	1	2	3	4	5	6	7
● Strategy	Easy to Manage					Complex to Manage	
● Process	Hierarchical Leadership					Distributed Leadership	
● IT Infrastructure	Closed and Proprietary					Open and Standards	
● People	Resource Management					Partnership Management	
● Culture/Change	Prescriptive					Self-Regulating	
● Measurement	Firm Shareholders					Value Chain Shareholders	

Figure 11–10
Governance and Collaboration

■ Bring in external experts trained in collaborative business models to discuss how to transform the organization and begin its transition to becoming more collaborative. Hire an experienced consulting firm to access the current c-commerce environment and establish a roadmap for the work process and moving forward the c-commerce initiative.

C-COMMERCE INTELLIGENCE QUOTIENT

Collaboration requires a sustained commitment to four major principles: (1) mutual relationships and goals, (2) joint development of structures with shared responsibilities, (3) joint authority and joint accountability for successful outcomes, and (4) shared resources and rewards. For an in-depth evaluation of c-commerce effectiveness, an assessment has been developed. Visit www.collaborationcommerce.com and complete a mini-diagnostic c-commerce intelligence assessment to gain additional insight and understand the most effective way to use limited resources. A more comprehensive assessment is available by contacting the author directly at info@collaborationcommerce.com. The questions correlate with the c-commerce framework: strategy, process, IT, people, culture, and measurement. See the appendix to learn more about the c-commerce intelligence quotient.

CONCLUSION

Understanding the c-commerce capabilities of the firm is an important first step to getting started. By identifying performance gaps, managers can develop the necessary actions to begin the shift forward. Never before in business history have relationships held such an important role in how we run our businesses, our organizations, and our nations. Given the transparency of the world we live in, c-commerce will impart the next competitive advantage.

Execution capabilities are rooted in the talent and quality of the people. Their abilities to create, innovate, and re-create through knowledge-sharing behaviors must be encouraged and unfettered. People will bring their best ideas and capabilities forward to help organizations innovate and grow only if they believe that by doing so they will be supported and rewarded for their actions. As competitive differentiation becomes increasingly difficult to maintain, it is the organization's people who will continue to supply its unique identity.

12

C-COMMERCE
QUICK REVIEW

Competition is accelerating across national boundaries at an
unprecedented pace. Consumers have more control and power
in the marketplace than they have had at any other time in
history. Using any one of many search engines on the Internet,
a customer can easily search for any product or service and
immediately find hundreds of choices, prices, and alternatives
from which to choose. This fundamental shift in consumer reach
has forced industries and firms to create more agile, adaptive,
and highly focused enterprises. In the coming decade, organizations will need to focus on three key areas:

- Leveraging networks as more and more enterprises strive
  for real-time c-commerce capabilities that remove latency
  from processes in support of more interconnected business
  models, which demand accurate and timely information.
- Changing business dynamics to achieve higher returns
  on investment and earnings per share via cost-cutting
  modified business models and a renewed focus on core
  competencies.
- Bringing people, information, and technology together in
  the form of collaborative customer and supplier portals,
  marketplaces, and fundamentally more open business
  models and application architectures.

Significant changes in perception create new realities; these changes are often driven by forces other than industry leaders. Open-source software development provides a good example of this dynamic. Leading software companies were not responsible for the current model, which involves the sharing of code used within software. Communities of developers collaborated informally and shared routines, lines of code, and best practices to create new processes and behaviors in the software industry. Software development firms had to provide new levels of detail, create online development environments, and share intellectual property to meet the needs of development communities. Research and development communities, even entire industries, are beginning to tap into intellectual property, publishing channels, knowledge sharing, and collaboration practices to innovate.

In an economy where information is a raw material and ideas are the commerce currency of knowledge exchange, relationships and networks enable information and ideas to be exchanged and innovation to be cultivated. The material presented throughout this book describes in detail how business dynamics are driven by people in collaborative networks; we refer to this process as c-commerce. Our research shows smaller firms are becoming able to quickly capture markets and excel within their industries by assembling and sharing skills and resources; it is this sharing of intellectual knowledge through critical networks of relationships using collaboration that imparts the competitive advantage. We present several mini-cases, or caselets, in each section of the book to illustrate how c-commerce is reshaping business ecosystems. The fact is this: *Increased collaboration is a fact of life in science, business, and markets. C-commerce is the next competitive advantage, and we are convinced that collaboration is the root of innovation practices.*

C-Commerce Overview

This book is structured in the following way: C-commerce fundamentals are presented in Part I. This section includes a definition and description of c-commerce and several caselets of how businesses throughout the world are responding to consumer demand and quickly changing marketplaces. Ten c-commerce capabilities are identified and described. Part II, the largest section of the book, discusses the c-commerce dimensions. We apply the ten c-commerce capabilities to seven organizational dimensions: governance, strategy, process, information technology infrastructure, people, culture and change, and measurement. Each dimension is looked at from traditional and c-commerce perspectives and illustrated with caselets. Part III covers c-commerce implementation paths and considerations. An assessment tool is provided to identify which of the ten c-commerce capabilities needs to be applied within each of the seven organizational dimensions. For the c-commerce capabilities and organizational dimensions that need to be focused on, specific activities are presented for consideration. (See Figure 12–1.) A summary of the book's chapters follows.

Chapter 1: C-Commerce Shift

This chapter outlines the purpose for writing the book and identifies the principal ideas that are to be discussed in detail throughout the book. Review this chapter for information about the following:

- *The early adopters.* What is being learned from early adopters and who is paying attention.
- *C-commerce and competitive advantage.* Changing the filters we use to look at business dynamics for the purpose of understanding how and why they are evolving.
- *C-commerce and timing.* Preparing for the future and engaging the next generation.
- *C-commerce and information infrastructure.* Leveraging technology and integrating supply chains.
- *Internal and external collaboration.* Leveraging networks.
- *Leading the change.* Several examples of forward thinking.
- *Organization of the book.* A short description of each chapter in the book.

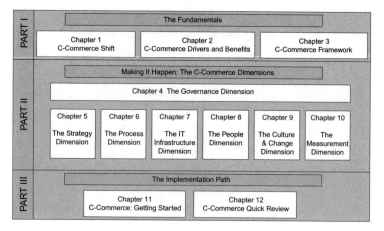

Figure 12–1
Review of the Book's Approach to C-Commerce

Chapter 2: C-Commerce Drivers and Benefits

Organizations are motivated to adopt a c-commerce approach. Chapter 2 identifies several drivers and their associated benefits. The benefits of c-commerce are supported by numerous short case studies. Review this chapter for information about the following:

- *Illustration of tangible benefits of c-commerce.* Examples include the following: emergence of intellectual property markets; meeting consumer and client demands; incorporating new behaviors, skills, and technologies; succeeding in ever riskier business environments; and accelerating innovation.
- *Case Study:* Billing and Settlement Processes in the U.S. Healthcare Industry
- *Case Study:* Cisco and FedEx
- *Case Study:* Toyota's Interorganizational Processes for Knowledge Transfer
- *Case Study:* Emergence of Intellectual Property (IP) Markets
- *Case Study:* Collaboration in the Aerospace and Copier Market Industries

Chapter 3: C-Commerce Framework

C-commerce is structured around ten core capabilities. Chapter 3 looks at how these capabilities are used to create collaboration that improves information and knowledge exchange and adds competitive value to diverse stakeholders. Review this chapter for information about the following:

- *The c-commerce capabilities:*
    1. Purpose—The driver
    2. Identity—The persona kaleidoscope
    3. Reputation—Character and image
    4. Trust—The core value
    5. Commerce—The knowledge flow
    6. Transparency—Informed and committed stakeholders
    7. Networks—The social nexus
    8. Boundaries—The rules
    9. Real-time collaboration enterprise (RTCE)—The adaptive organization
    10. Governance—Make and execute decisions

Chapter 4: The Governance Dimension

Governance provides the necessary organizational support to achieve the c-commerce vision. Review this chapter for information about the following:

- *Governance and levers of c-commerce.* Governance shifts in strategy, process, information technology infrastructure, people, culture and change, and measurement from traditional approaches to c-commerce approaches are outlined.
- *Critical issues for c-commerce.* Areas to address include licensing, contracting, and supporting operating principles; the role of leadership and ongoing reflection and learning; and change management and communication channels.
- *Case Study:* Visa
- *Case Study:* The Counterexample: GSTPA and Straight Through Processing

Chapter 5: The Strategy Dimension

The strategy enables the firm to define the mission of c-commerce and establish the approach to deliver results. Establish a primary driver or focal point to ensure that c-commerce objectives are aligned. Review this chapter for information about the following:

- *Strategy and c-commerce capabilities.* The major shifts from traditional approaches to c-commerce approaches are outlined.
- *Finding and communicating a unique strategy.* The c-commerce strategy will have a primary driver. Examples include cost, focus, flexibility, and customer intimacy.
- *Case Study:* Kryptonite Bike Lock Firm
- *Case Study:* JetBlue

Chapter 6: The Process Dimension

Business process management is a means of reducing cost, improving quality, optimizing the use of business resources and management attention, and becoming more agile in responding to new opportunities and changes in the marketplace. C-commerce incentives are to innovate, improve, and maintain business process performance at world-class levels. Review this chapter for information about the following:

- *Process and c-commerce capabilities.* The major shifts from traditional approaches to c-commerce approaches are outlined.
- *The value proposition.* Use the primary driver of the c-commerce strategy as a lens through which to assess c-commerce capabilities and apply them to the variety of work types across the firm.
- *Case Study:* Cisco Improves Supply Chain

Chapter 7: The Information Technology Infrastructure Dimension

Consider the firm's effectiveness in its ability to optimize information technology (IT) infrastructure and share information across business units, among partners, and within the firm. These interactions need to be focused on improving shareholder value through a shared IT architecture, open source, applications, systems, services, and business processes. Review this chapter for information about the following:

- *IT infrastructure and c-commerce capabilities.* The major shifts from traditional approaches to c-commerce approaches are outlined.
- *SMART Web.* The design and architecture of an IT enabling framework. The first letters of these attributes spell the word *smart:* seamless, measurable, access and integration, real-enough time, and transparent.
- *Delivery models.* Distinct types of communication are needed for c-commerce to be effective for individuals, teams, and functions.
- *Case Study:* Use of C-Commerce Capabilities in Research and Development
- *Case Study:* Open Source Product Development

Chapter 8: The People Dimension

People are the foundation of the firm's social nexus and define the current and future value of relationship networks in the organization. Who we know (relationship capital) is frequently more important than what we know (human capital). C-commerce provides the ability to capitalize and maximize the combined human capital and relationship capital solution, creating both innovation and improvement. Review this chapter for information about the following:

- *People and c-commerce capabilities.* The major shifts from traditional approaches to c-commerce approaches are outlined.
- *Developing guidelines.* Establish standards and guidelines to design relationship management into work processes, assign the same team to design processes and manage relationships, focus on knowledge-transfer activities, and manage virtual teams.
- *Case Study:* Volvo—Supply Chain Collaboration Case Summary

- *Case Study:* McKinsey
- *Case Study:* Linked In—A Social Networking Business Model

Chapter 9: The Culture and Change Dimension

In preparing for c-commerce, it is important to analyze the differences between the current culture and the vision of the future culture. Understanding how work is currently done with respect to formal and informal networks provides strategic insights to the health of collaboration capabilities. Attention should be paid to explicit differences in organizational practices, such as how work is distributed and how decisions are made; these are key performance indicators. Be certain that differences in culture can be bridged as part of a c-commerce initiative. Review this chapter for information about the following:

- *Culture, change, and c-commerce capabilities.* The major shifts from traditional approaches to c-commerce approaches are outlined.
- *Case Study:* McKinsey Alumni Database—Leveraging Brand and Networks
- *Case Study:* EBay—Cultural Values and Community Respect
- *Case Study:* View22—Seeing the Big Picture

Chapter 10: The Measurement Dimension

Performance management has shifted organizations from a command-and-control model of leadership to a facilitation model. The scope of measurement begins with a clear insight on whom the users are, what metrics are associated with the processes that they manage, and what logic or rules apply when analyzing the status and effectiveness of these processes. Review this chapter for information about the following:

- *Measurement and c-commerce capabilities.* The major shifts from traditional approaches to c-commerce approaches are outlined.

- *Selecting critical measures.* Traditional accounting measures do not meet the complete measurement needs of the firm. C-commerce requires firms to look at a collection of measurements to focus and improve the use of business processes that support performance capital and relationship capital.
- *Case Study:* Supply Chain Collaboration and Demand Forecasting

Chapter 11: C-Commerce: Getting Started

Suggested improvement activities to consider are available for each of the ten c-commerce capabilities. Each suggestion offers ways to improve collaboration and the flow of information and knowledge exchange. Review this chapter for information about the following:

- *Getting started with the c-commerce capabilities:*
  1. Purpose
     - Expand the organization's strategy to clearly include and communicate a purpose that supports the network (social and IT) goals and objectives.
     - Make certain that people understand how the tasks they perform map to the firm's purpose.
  2. Identity
     - Focus on knowledge-management activities and best practices.
     - Create an identity management program.
  3. Reputation
     - Update the strategy and communication plans to include specific activities and tasks to successfully manage the complexity of a c-commerce organization.
     - Establish a rapid application development environment within the IT infrastructure to quickly respond to and implement change.
  4. Trust
     - Monitor employee attitude and work to reduce conflict and confusion in communications, thus improving and increasing reciprocity.

- Make certain the firm's remuneration and recognition program rewards sharing information and knowledge.

5. Commerce
   - Assess how information and knowledge are exchanged in teams and throughout the inter- and intraorganizational business processes.
   - Make certain business processes are driven by customer relationships and supply chain goals and objectives.

6. Transparency
   - Add a work process and c-commerce initiative into an existing program.
   - Design and deploy an enterprise portal that can be personalized to meet the needs of employees, customers, partners, and others.

7. Networks
   - Focus on relationship network activities and best practices using virtual teams to complete projects.
   - Leverage social networking analytic approaches to evaluate the health of networks.

8. Boundaries
   - Design and implement an open business intelligence program that tracks c-commerce key performance indicators.
   - Change executive leadership C-level roles that demonstrate desired behavior.

9. Real-Time Collaboration Enterprise
   - Establish a business process management program.
   - Increase integration of the IT infrastructure.

10. Governance
    - Position an executive accountable for collaborative business strategies.
    - Bring in external experts trained in collaborative business models to discuss how to transform and transition the organization to become more collaborative.

Chapter 12: C-Commerce Quick Review

This chapter provides a quick summary and overview of the book. It is a reference to recap the key points for those who want to gain a quick understanding of where to locate topics addressed in the book.

CONCLUSION

Leaders are accountable for adjusting to new business demands, models, and market dynamics. This book is designed to help prepare leaders to develop their strategies and migration plans to take advantage of collaborative business models. Leaders will be equipped with an understanding of how important this fundamental business shift is, combined with a practical operational context on what is rapidly evolving. C-commerce business models are achievable, but they require commitment and change across a number of business capability areas: governance, strategy, process design, information technology infrastructure, people management, culture and change, and measurement.

There are several keys to the successful adoption of c-commerce in the firm and across the value chain: Focus on core capabilities; create a strategic initiative (rather than a tactical solution); integrate and change corporate culture; foster open and constructive learning dialogue; preserve information relationship networks; establish knowledge connections; foster communities; enforce IT infrastructure standards; improve data integration; improve planning processes; focus on win-win solutions; and shift to deeper integrated reward and recognition systems to align with c-commerce goals.

An important characteristic of the drive toward c-commerce is the undisputed value of network effects on the ability of an organization to grow exponentially and to generate above-average returns. Collaborative networks create new value possibilities for the whole ecosystem of enterprises involved in a value chain. The issue is not about economies of scale or scope; it is about leverage—how every player in the ecosystem can leverage each other's information, knowledge, skills, contacts, and brand into multiple win-win situations. In the past, companies shared mainly physical resources; now the key is sharing knowledge, which can build more intelligent organizations or, from a network perspective, build a collective intelligence.

The logic is inescapable: collaborative business models and collaborative leaders are needed because globalization forces have made the talent market bigger, more powerful, and more competitive. We live in an ideas-based economy in which c-commerce is the next competitive advantage. Every organization or nation wants to grow and innovate. However, approaches to achieving these common goals vary dramatically from enterprise to enterprise and nation to nation. Creative approaches are needed to overcome these differences.

We hope this book is an inspiration to executives and provides useful frameworks and ideas to help apply c-commerce effectively in the organization. Relationships take on a new meaning in c-commerce and create a new form of capital. C-commerce is about the next sustainable competitive advantage. Be prepared.

Appendix

C-Commerce Intelligence Assessment

For centuries, armies, nations, governments, and businesses have depended on collaboration to progress and survive. Nevertheless, many current organizational practices and methods of thinking do not acknowledge or take advantage of collaborative opportunities. Facts reinforcing the importance of collaboration include the following:

- Fifty percent of Fortune 500 companies seldom survive more than 50 years; the primary cause for their demise is lack of community integration to develop resilient and adaptive and learning practices (Stewart 2003).
- The ability to learn faster is the only competitive edge remaining (Senge 2003, de Geus 2001).

Stories abound concerning best practices in collaboration. Bob Buckman, retired president of Buckman Labs, invested heavily in collaboration practices. For many years, Buckman Labs spent more than $8 million annually in collaboration and knowledge intensive approaches to support its business. By

231

investing in collaboration, Buckman Labs was able to more than double the introduction of new products from 14% of sales to 34%. Core values focused on creating an improved climate of trust and an increased willingness to collaborate.

Too many organizations in both the for-profit and not-for-profit sectors fail to follow such examples. The result is a lack of effective collaboration. We have developed the C-Commerce Intelligence Quotient to help our clients assess and take advantage of their strengths and reduce their gaps in c-commerce.

Parallel to the structure of this book, we have developed a series of questions that relate to our consistent working definitions of c-commerce. The questions examine c-commerce within the context of strategy, process, information technology, people, culture, and measurement. Each of these core competencies needs to be carefully assessed, and, as gaps are identified, systemic programs need to be developed to help your organization to further evolve into a stronger collaborative and relationship intelligent organization.

Visit our Web site at www.collaborationcommerce.com to complete a mini-diagnostic c-commerce intelligence assessment. A more comprehensive assessment is available by contacting us directly at info@collaborationcommerce.com.

Heidi Collins has more than 25 years of experience as a consultant, knowledge manager, business process analyst, information architect, and leading expert on enterprise portal solutions. She speaks on knowledge management and enterprise portals for organizations throughout the world.

As a writer, Collins has published *Corporate Portals* (AMACOM 2001). The book provides a clear, practical, and detailed picture of the technical and organizational issues involved in creating a corporate portal solution. Her second book, *Enterprise Knowledge Portals* (AMACOM 2003), describes the intersection of knowledge management and the enterprise portal and covers the components of knowledge management strategies, including locating information, learning while doing, capturing human expertise, and reusing information. She can be reached at hcollins@ptd.net.

Dr. Cindy Gordon is the chief executive officer and founder of Helix Commerce International Inc. (www.helixcommerce.com). Her firm specializes in business innovation and growth acceleration services, including business innovation strategy, mergers and acquisitions, customer relationship management, complexity management, and collaboration commerce business models leveraging third-generation knowledge management and e-commerce solutions. She speaks internationally in these areas, and has authored more than four books. Her most recent book, *Realizing the Promise of Corporate Portals: Leveraging Knowledge for Business Success* (Elsevier 2003), was published with co-author José Cláudio Terra. She has held senior executive positions with Citicorp, Nortel Networks, Accenture, and Xerox. She also is a board director and board advisor to many leading collaboration and e-commerce companies, including Bubble Labs, Cquay, QuickPlay Media, Snipe Networks, View22, and Zymeta. She can be reached at cindy@helixcommerce.com.

José Cláudio C. Terra, Ph.D., is the chief executive officer of TerraForum, a leading consulting firm specializing in knowledge management, innovation management, and corporate portals. In recent years, Terra has held management and executive positions in large business and media organizations such as Organic, Rogers, Globo Cabo, and Editoria Abril in Canada and Brazil. Terra has published widely in English and Portuguese on business strategy, knowledge management, innovation, creativity, managing research and development, and industrial and technology policy. His first book, *Knowledge Management: The Great Business Challenge*, is an enormous success in Brazil and is in its fifth edition, and *Corporate Portals: The Revolution in Knowledge Management* was released worldwide and has been recommended by Harvard Business School. In 2003 he published two new books, *Knowledge Management in Small and Medium Enterprises* and *Knowledge Management and E-Learning in Practice*, both in Portuguese, and also contributed chapters to collections published in the United States and Portugal. He can be reached at jcterra@terraforum.com.br or through www.terraforum.com.br or www.terraforum.ca.

BIBLIOGRAPHY

Allen S, Bassi L, McMurrer D. Human capital: how's your return on people? *Harvard Business Review,* March 2004.

Allen S, Teten D, Fisher D. *Five Keys to Building Relationships Online.* eBook: Onlinebusinessnetworks.com, 2004.

Ambrose C, Morello D. "Designing the Agile Organization: Design Principles and Practices." Gartner Strategic Analysis Report, January 2004.

Ballow JJ, Thomas RJ, Roos G. *Future Value: The $7 Trillion Challenge.* New York: Accenture, 2004.

Barr JG. *Web Conferencing Market Trends.* Pennsauken, NJ: Faulkner Information Services, 2004.

Barret L, Schwaber CE. Firms can improve success rate by learning from open source software development. *Computer Weekly,* June 2004.

Bassett G. Business intelligence for corporate information assets. *DM Direct,* March 2002.

Bassi LJ, Harrison P, Ludwig J, McMurrer DP. Human capital investments and firm performance. *Human Capital Dynamics,* 2001.

Bassi LJ, Ludwig J, McMurrer DP, Buren MV. "Profiting from Learning: Do Firms' Investments in Education and Training Pay Off?" ASTD/Saba White Paper, 2000.

Bassi LJ, McGraw K, McMurrer D. "Beyond Quarterly Earnings: Using Measurement to Create Sustainable Growth." McBassi and Company White Paper, September 2003.

Bassi LJ, McGraw K, McMurrer D. "Make Measurement Your Ally." McBassi and Company White Paper, May 2002.

239

Bassi LJ, McGraw K, McMurrer D. "A New Kind of Measurement System." McBassi and Company White Paper, June 2003.

Battell J. Why blogs mean business. *Business 2.0*, February 2004.

Baxley C, Roberts B, Jarvenpaa SL. Evolving at the speed of change: the journey toward mastery of change at Motorola's semiconductor products sector. *MIS Quarterly*, 2003.

BEA Systems. *Application Platform Suites: An Architectural Cost Analysis*. San Jose, CA: BEA, 2003.

Bell M. "Building and Supporting the Agile Workplace." Gartner Symposium IT XPO, October 2003.

Bender E. Rules of the collaboratory game. *MIT Enterprise Technology Review*, November 2004.

Bodley J. *Cultural Anthropology: Tribes, Stages, and Global Systems*. New York: Free Press, 1994.

Boeing Corp. *Computing & Design/Build Processes Help Develop the 777*. Chicago: Boeing, 2005.

Bontis N. "Intellectual Capital Trends." McMaster Intellectual Capital Conference, January 2005.

Bontis N, Gordon C. Measuring enterprise risk and intangible assets. *KM World*, 2004.

Bruce A, Langdon K. *Project Management*. New York: Dorling Kindersley Publishing, 2000.

Bruce A, Langdon K. *Strategic Thinking*. New York: Dorling Kindersley Publishing, 2000.

Bryan LL. Making a market in knowledge: for companies and their employees alike knowledge is power—and profit. *The McKinsey Quarterly*, no. 3, 2004.

Burke RM. *Appreciative Inquiry: A Literature Review*. Cleveland: Appreciative Inquiry Commons, 2001.

Burlton R. *Business Process Management: Profiting from Process*. Indianapolis: Sams, 2001.

Business World Online. Cisco improves supply chain system. *Business World Online*, March 12, 2001.

Chris A, Morello D. "Designing the Agile Organization: Principles and Practices." Gartner Symposium IT XPO, October 2003.

Clemmer J. Bridging the credibility gap. *Globe and Mail*, February 4, 2005.

Collins H. *Corporate Portal: Revolutionizing Information Access to Increase Productivity and Drive the Bottom Line*. New York: AMACOM, 2001.

Collins H. *Enterprise Knowledge Portals: Next-Generation Portal Solutions for Dynamic Information Access, Better Decision Making, and Maximum Results.* New York: AMACOM, 2003.

Collins JC, Porras JI. *Built to Last: Successful Habits of Visionary Companies.* New York: HarperCollins Publishers, 1997.

Coulson-Thomas C. *Negotiating Partnering Relationships: From Confrontation to Collaboration.* Manchester: Saferpak, 2004.

Craig A. "Bentley Unveils VIECON Internet Strategy to Integrate Communications, Collaboration, Commerce for Engineering/Construction/Operations Networks." Daratech.com, June 2000.

Cunningham & Cunningham, Inc. "Front Page." http://c2.com, September 2004.

Cunningham & Cunningham, Inc. "People, Projects and Patterns." http://c2.com, October 2004.

Cunningham & Cunningham, Inc. "Purpose of Patterns." http://c2.com, October 2004.

Dafermos GN. Management and virtual decentralized networks: the linux project. *First Monday,* June 2001.

Dalton et al. *Globalizing Industry Research and Development.* Washington, D.C.: Bureau of Economic Analysis, U.S. Department of Commerce, 2003.

de Geus A, Senge P. *The Living Company.* Boston: Harvard Business Press, 1997.

Deloitte. *Mastering Innovation: Exploiting Ideas for Profitable Growth.* New York: Deloitte, 2004.

Deutschman A. Change or die. *Fast Company,* May 2005.

de Ramo A. The China syndrome. *CFO Magazine,* 2003.

Di Maio A. "ROI in Government: Toward the Public Value of IT." Gartner Symposium IT XPO, October 2003.

Dunbar R. Thinking out loud. *CIO Insight,* October 2, 2002.

Dyer JH, Hatch NW. Using supplier networks to learn faster. *Sloan Management Review,* Spring 2004.

Dysart J. Conversations and communities. *KM World.* May 2004.

e-Content Institute. *The Age.* Toronto: e-Content Institute, 2004.

eMarketplace. Promoting collaborative trading. *Sun Microsystems,* 2004.

Engineering/Construction/Operations Industry in Technology Transition. Daratech.com, June 2000.

Ericson J. E-Business ecosystem. *Portals Magazine,* February 2004.

Estrada J. Driving revenue through collaboration: financial services firms prepare for market upswing. *KM World*, October 2003.

Factiva Inc. *Deriving Order from Chaos: The Benefits of an Information Integration Strategy*. Toronto: Factiva, 2004.

Faiello P. *Employee Power*. Toronto: CA Magazine, 2000.

Falcett M. "Lessons Learned: Deploying Manager Self Service at Pitney Bowes." The HR Service Delivery Forum 2004, May 2004.

Flint D. How to make managerial processes part of business fusion. *Gartner Research Note*, January 2004.

Goldbert AI, Cohen GF. Reputation building: small business strategies for successful venture development. *Journal of Small Business Management*, April 1, 2003.

Gramann C, Barbara G. Content management. *BI Report*, February 2002.

Greenleaf R. *Servant Leadership: A Journey into the Nature of Legitimate Power and Greatness*. Mahwah, NJ: Paulist Press, 1977.

Heller R. *Managing Teams*. New York: Dorling Kindersley Publishing, 1998.

Hobbs M. Increasing your enterprise IQ. *DM Direct*, October 2000.

Holtz S. "Sustaining Momentum During Challenging Times." Corporate Communications and Technology Conference, September 2004.

Hope-Ross D. "Supplier Relationship Management and Contracts Management: Building Value in Supplier Relationships." Gartner Symposium IT XPO, October 2003.

Hourihan M. What we're doing when we blog. *O'Reilly Web Devcenter*, June 13, 2002.

Hughes M. *Launching Successful Projects*. Austin, TX: Terraquest Metrics, 2004.

Infoconomy. Business process management: an executive guide to BPM. *Infoconomy*, February 7, 2004.

Issacs B. Dialogue as a business process and effective conversations. *The Systems Thinker*, 2003.

Kaihla P. Nokia's hit factory. *Business 2.0*, August 2002.

Kanter R et al. *Innovation: Breakthrough Thinking at 3M, DuPont, GE, Pfizer, and Rubbermaid*. New York: Harper Business, 1997.

Katcher B. *DiscoverySurveys.com*. 2005.

Keeley L. *The Taming of the New*. Boston: Harvard Business School Press, 2004.

KM Technologies. *Value of Collaboration and Document Management*. Montreal: KM Technologies, 2004.

KM World. Best practices in enterprise content management. *KM World*, March 2004.

KM World. Best practices in enterprise knowledge management. *KM World*, December 2004.

Knopman D et al. *Innovation and Change Management in Public and Private Organizations*. Santa Monica, CA: RAND Documented Briefing, 2003.

Krebs V. Knowledge networks: mapping and measuring knowledge creation, reuse, and flow. *Orgnet.com*, 1998.

Krebs V. Managing the connected organization, *Orgnet.com*, 1999.

Krebs V. Power in networks. *Orgnet.com*, 2004.

Krebs V, June H. Building sustainable communities through network building. *Orgnet.com*, 2002.

Kroeber AL. The superorganic. *American Anthropologist*, 1917.

Kroeber, AL. *Anthropology: Race, Language, Culture, Psychology, Prehistory*. New York: Brace and World Publishers, 1948.

Latham L. "The New Generation of Real-Time Collaboration." Gartner Symposium IT XPO, October 2003.

MacMillan I, McGrath RG. Using discovery-driven planning in business building. *e-Newsletter for Wharton Executive Education*, October 2002.

Mahowald RP. Collaboration. *eINFORM*, 2002.

Majchrzak A, Malhotra A. *Deploying Far-Flung Teams: A Guidebook for Managers*. Chicago: Society for Information Management Advanced Practices Council, 2003.

Majchrzak A, Malhotra A. *Virtual Workspace Technology Use and Knowledge-Sharing Effectiveness in Distributed Teams: The Influence of a Team's Transactive Memory*. Chicago: Information Systems Research, 2004.

McGregor J. It's a blog world after all. *Fast Company*, April 2004.

McMillan G. Still building houses of cards? Part 1. *BI Report*, June 2002.

McMillan G. Still building houses of cards? Part 2: The vision for an enterprise center of excellence. *DM Direct*, June 2002.

Michel J. Enterprise-wide online working environment. *DM Direct*, April 2003.

Mongoose Technology. *The 12 Principles of Collaboration*. Houston, TX: Mongoose, 2002.

National Science Board. *Science and Engineering Indicators*. Arlington, VA: National Science Board, 2004.

Oestreich D, Ryan K. *Driving Fear Out of the Workplace*. San Francisco: Jossey-Bass Publishers, 1998.

Pascoe D. Four secrets to online success revealed. *DM Direct*, February 2004.

Pearson J. Can social networks serve business? *Information Highways*, June 2004.

Quinn JB. Outsourcing innovation: the new engine for growth. *Sloan Management Review*, Summer 2000.

Rampersad H, Leonard D. *Total Performance Scorecard: Redefining Management to Achieve Performance with Integrity*. Boston: Butterworth-Heinemann, 2002.

Raskino M. Take a real-world view of real time. *Gartner Research Note*, January 2004.

RNEP. *Projeto Giga*. Rio de Janeiro: Rede Nacional de Ensino e Pesquisa, 2005.

Rutten R. *Knowledge and Innovation in Regional Industry: An Entrepreneurial Coalition*. New York: Routledge, 2003.

Rycroft R. *Self-Organizing Innovation Networks: Implications for Globalization*. Washington, D.C.: Elliott School of International Affairs, George Washington University, 2003.

Rycroft R. *Technology-Based Globalization Indicators: The Centrality of Innovation Network Data*. Washington, D.C.: George Washington University, 2002.

Saint-Onge H, Wallace D. *Leveraging Strategic Communities of Practice*. Boston: Butterworth-Heinemann, 2003.

Sagey B. *Solutions for Managing Unstructured Enterprise Data*. Pennsauken, NJ: Faulkner Information Services, 2004.

SAP. *Implementing Collaborative Knowledge Networks with SAP NetWeaver*. Walldorf, Germany: SAP AG, 2004.

Schorr L. *Common Purpose: Strengthening Families and Neighborhoods to Rebuild America*. New York: Anchor Books, 1997.

Schulte R, Natis Y. "The Agile Enterprise: Service-Oriented and Event-Driven." Gartner Symposium IT XPO, October 2003.

Schumann M. "Understanding the New Rules for Workforce Engagement: Finding the Clues in Research." Corporate Communications and Technology Conference, September 2004.

Schwarz E. Sparking the fire of invention. *Technology Review*, May 2004.

Senge P. *The Fifth Discipline*. New York: Doubleday, 1990.

Senge P et al. *The Fifth Discipline Fieldbook*. New York: Doubleday, 1994.

SIBIS. Internet for R&D. *SIBIS*, December 2003.

Stranger P, Hemerling J. West meets East. *Canadian Business Report*, January 2005.

Stratigos A, Strouse R. The library of the future. *Online*, January/February 2003.

Sterman J. Building Communities of Commitment. *The Systems Thinker*, January 1995.

Stewart T. *Intellectual Capital: The New Wealth of Organizations*. New York: Doubleday, 1997.

Tapscott D. Sharing leads to abundance. *Intelligent Enterprise*, September 1, 2003.

Teece D, Pisano G. The Dynamic Capabilities of Firms: An Introduction. In *Technology, Organization, and Competitiveness Perspectives on Industrial and Corporate Change*, edited by David Teece, Giovanni Dois, Josef Chytry. Oxford University Press, 1998.

The Economist. An open-source shot in the arm? *The Economist Technology Quarterly*, June 10, 2004.

The Economist. Reinventing Europe. *The Economist Technology Quarterly*, September 4, 2003.

UGS PLM Solutions. *Teamcenter Community: Real-Time Product Collaboration on Every Desktop*. Portland, OR: UGS, 2004.

UGS PLM Solutions. *Procter and Gamble Creates a Collaborative Community*. Portland, OR: UGS, 2004.

University of California. *Job Description and Strategic Plan*. San Diego: USCD Human Resources Department, 2000.

University of California. *Managing Team Performance: Definitions*. San Diego: USCD Human Resources Department, 2000.

University of California. *Observation and Feedback*. San Diego: USCD Human Resources Department, 2000.

University of California. *Overview of Performance Management*. San Diego: USCD Human Resources Department, 2000.

University of California. *Performance Appraisal*. San Diego: USCD Human Resources Department, 2000.

University of California. *Performance Development Plan*. San Diego: USCD Human Resources Department, 2000.

University of California. *Standards of Performance*. San Diego: USCD Human Resources Department, 2000.

University of Western Australia. *Towards a Definition of Online Learning at UWA*. Perth: Centre for the Advancement of Teaching and Learning, 2003.

Werbach K. Spectrum wants to be free. *Wired Magazine,* January 2003.

Wall Street & Technology. The fat lady sings: GSTPA to dissolve. *Wall Street & Technology,* November 22, 2002.

White L. *The Science of Culture*. New York: Grove Press, 1949.

INDEX

Purpose, 134–135, 206–207
  to diversity, 158–160
  driver, 34–36
  from firm centric, 109–110
  from firm versus firm, 67–69
  to goals, 134–135
  from independent, 185–187
  to network versus network, 67–69
  from products and services, 85–87
  to relationship-centric processes,
    85–87
  to shared and agile, 185–187
  from tasks, 134–135
  from uniformity, 158–160
  to value chain centric, 109–110

Q
Quick review, 219–230

R
Real-time collaboration enterprise, 145,
    173–174, 196–197, 215–216
  from cautious and methodical, 173–174
  to curious and adaptive, 173–174
  to dynamic, 196–197
  to dynamic and iterative, 96
  to fast and iterative, 75–76
  to multi-dimensional, 145
  from one-to-one, one-to-many, and
    asynchronous, 120–121
  to one-to-one, one-to-many, and
    synchronous, 120–121
  from sequential, 96
  from single dimensional, 145
  from slow and cyclical, 75–76
  from static, 196–197
Reflection and learning, ongoing, 59–61
Relationship management, 149
Relationships
  among many diverse stakeholders, 9
  managing, 149–150
Reputation, 188–189, 208–209
  to agile and flexible, 111
  character and image, 37–38
  from closed, 188–189
  to complex-to-manage, 69–71
  to comprehensive, 162–163
  to customer relationships, 89–90
  damaged, 70–71
  from easy-to-manage, 69–71
  from individual, 138–139
  from narrow, 162–163
  to network, 138–139
  to open, 188–189

from product experience, 89–90
from reliable and specific, 111
Research and development, c-commerce
  capabilities in, 127–129
Review, quick, 219–230
RTCE (real-time collaboration enterprise),
  44–45
Rules, 43–44

S
Shift, c-commerce, 3–14, 221–222
SMART Web, 121–126
  access, 124–125
  integration, 124–125
  measurable, 123–124
  real-enough time, 125
  seamless, 122–123
  transparent, 125–126
Social networking business model,
  154–155
Social nexus, 42–43
Stakeholders, 41–42
Started, getting, 205–218, 227–228
  boundaries, 214–215
  c-commerce intelligence quotient, 217
  commerce, 210–211
  governance, 216–217
  identity, 207–208
  networks, 213–214
  purpose, 206–207
  real-time collaboration enterprise,
    215–216
  reputation, 208–209
  transparency, 211–212
  trust, 209–210
Strategy
  to customer first, 55
  finding unique, 77–81
  from firm first, 55
Strategy dimension, 66–84, 224
  boundaries, 74–75
  commerce, 72–73
  governance, 76–77
  identity, 69
  networks, 74
  purpose, 67–69
  real-time collaboration enterprise,
    75–76
  reputation, 69–71
  transparency, 73
  trust, 71–72
Supplier associations, 21
Supply chain collaboration, 152–153,
  200–201

S65494

DH

658
COL

5000629427

ax